EDGARTOWN
Free Public Library

THE GREATEST OF ALL our American institutions is our system of public libraries. No country has anything like it. If you've tried to do research or work with libraries overseas and abroad you are immediately reminded how fortunate we are. We just take it for granted.
— David McCullough

Presented by

26 West Tisbury Road
Edgartown, Mass. 02539

THE
PASSAGEWAY

the Bone Orchard
MYTHOS

IMAGE COMICS, INC. • Robert Kirkman: Chief Operating Officer • Erik Larsen: Chief Financial Officer • Todd McFarlane: President • Marc Silvestri: Chief Executive Officer • Jim Valentino: Vice President • Eric Stephenson: Publisher / Chief Creative Officer • Nicole Lapalme: Controller • Leanna Caunter: Accounting Analyst • Sue Korpela: Accounting & HR Manager • Marla Eizik: Talent Liaison • Jeff Boison: Director of Sales & Publishing Planning • Lorelei Bunjes: Director of Digital Services • Dirk Wood: Director of International Sales & Licensing • Alex Cox: Director of Direct Market Sales • Chloe Ramos: Book Market & Library Sales Manager • Emilio Bautista: Digital Sales Coordinator • Jon Schlaffman: Specialty Sales Coordinator • Kat Salazar: Director of PR & Marketing • Monica Garcia: Marketing Design Manager • Drew Fitzgerald: Marketing Content Associate • Heather Doornink: Production Director • Drew Gill: Art Director • Hilary DiLoreto: Print Manager • Tricia Ramos: Traffic Manager • Melissa Gifford: Content Manager • Erika Schnatz: Senior Production Artist • Ryan Brewer: Production Artist • Deanna Phelps: Production Artist • IMAGECOMICS.COM

Publication design by Steve Wands

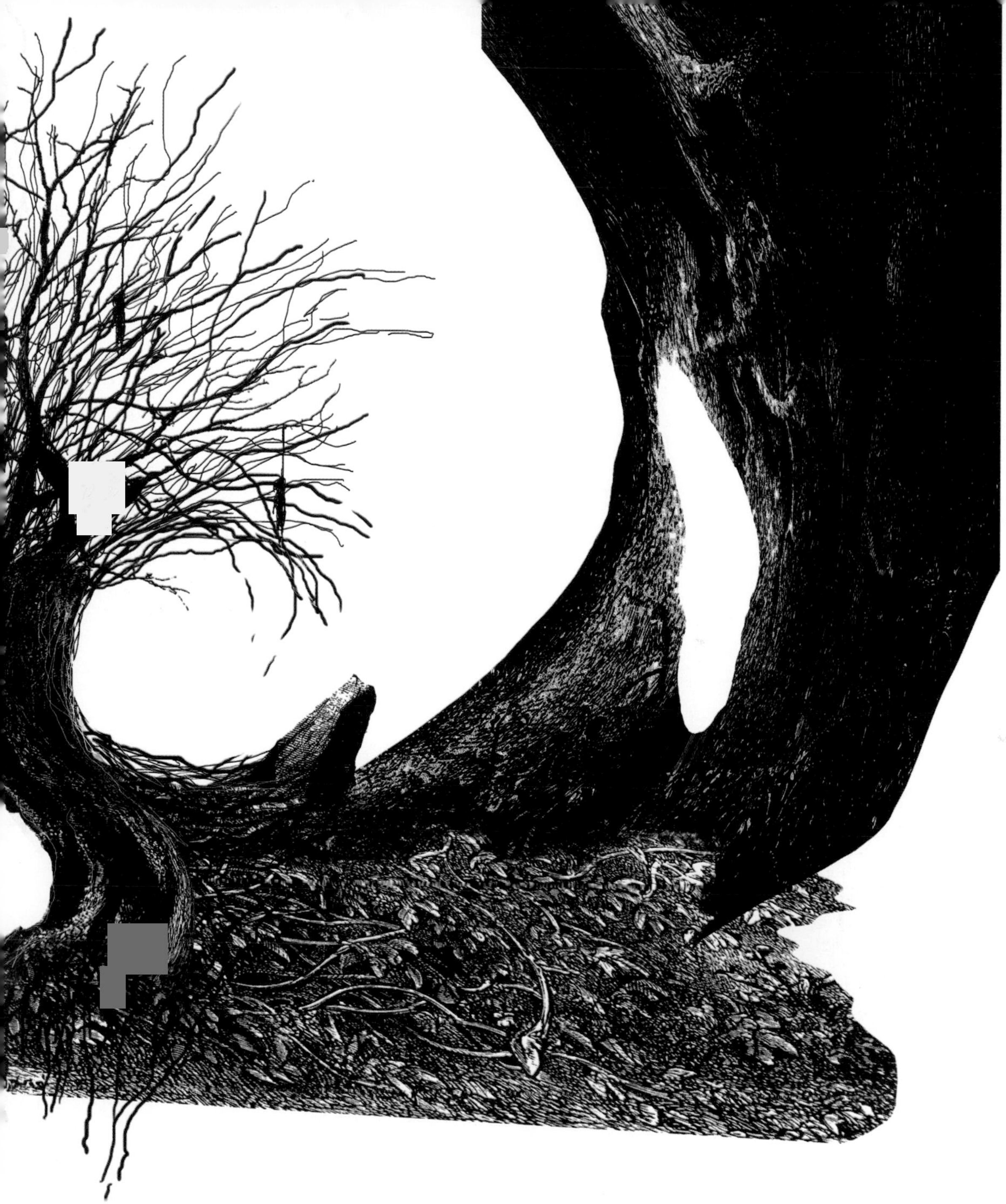

JEFF LEMIRE
ANDREA SORRENTINO
DAVID STEWART colorist
STEVE WANDS letterer & designer
GREG LOCKARD editor

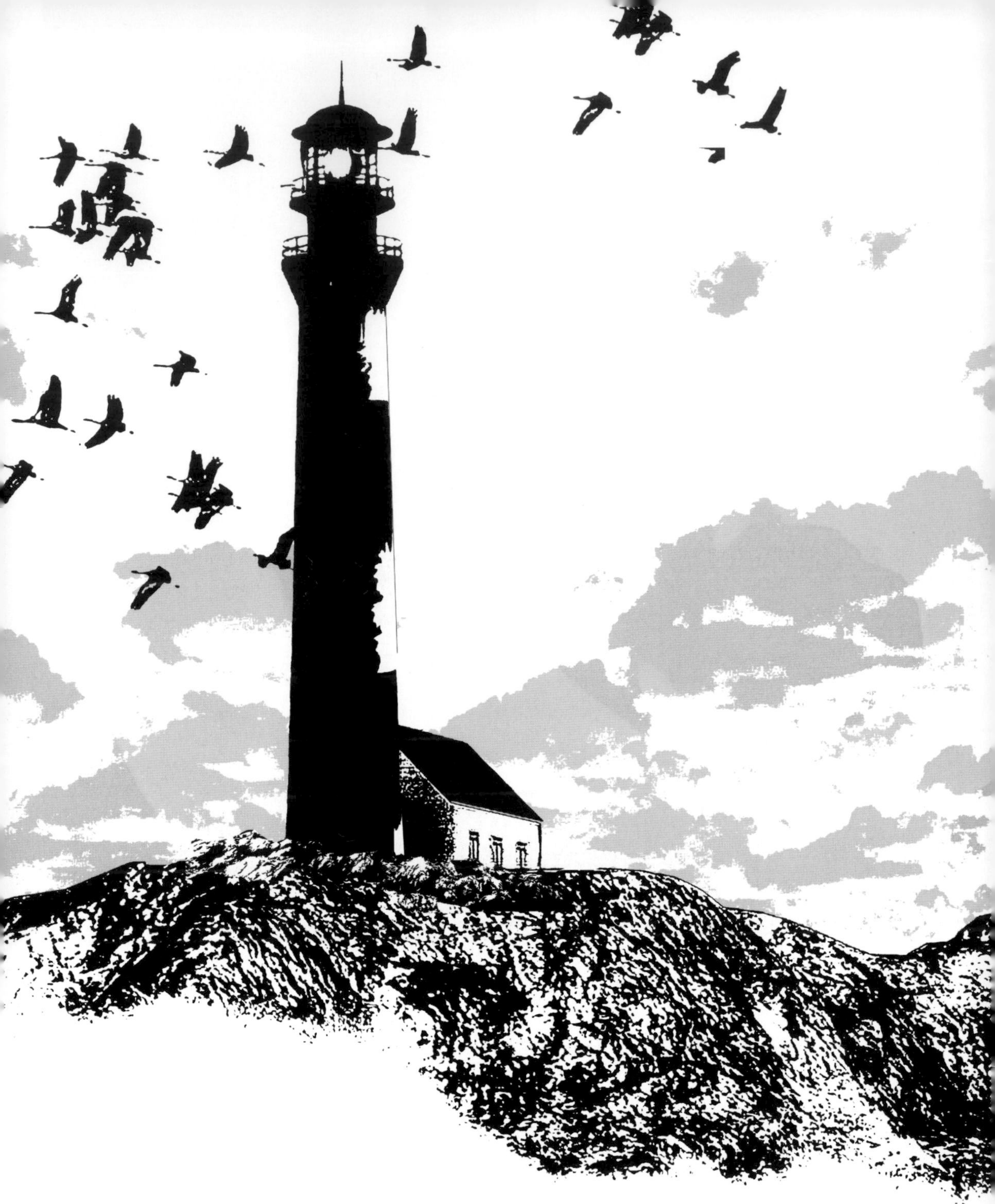

I SAW MY MOTHER LAST NIGHT.

SHE HAD THAT **SAME LOOK** ON HER FACE...

EXCEPT FOR **HER EYES.**

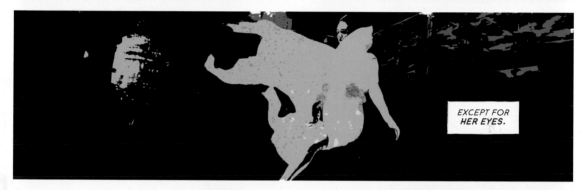

WHY WERE HER EYES GONE? WHAT--WHAT **TOOK THEM?**

I CAN'T THINK ABOUT THAT.

I CAN'T THINK ABOUT **WHAT** TOOK HER EYES.

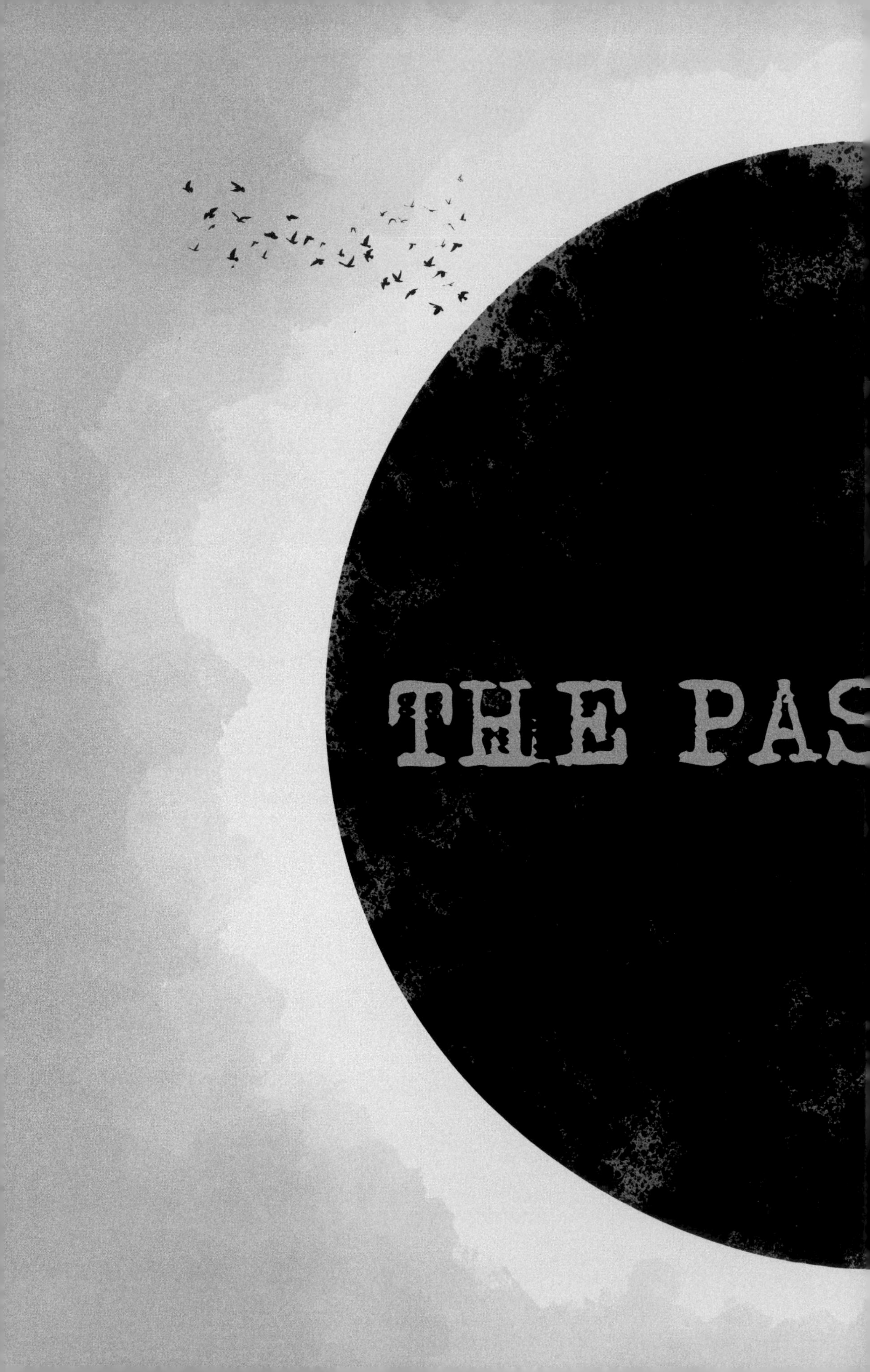
THE PAS

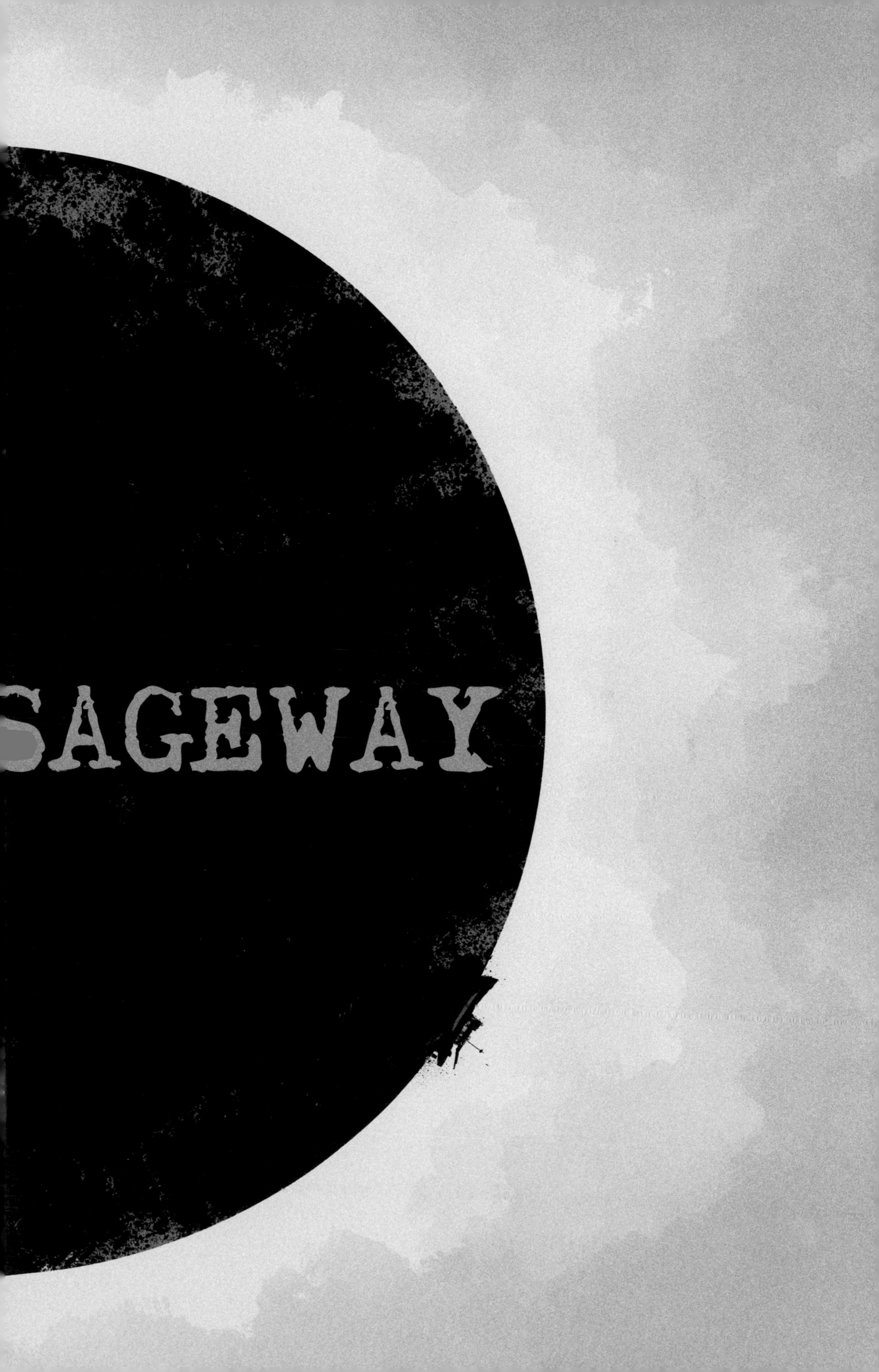
SAGEWAY

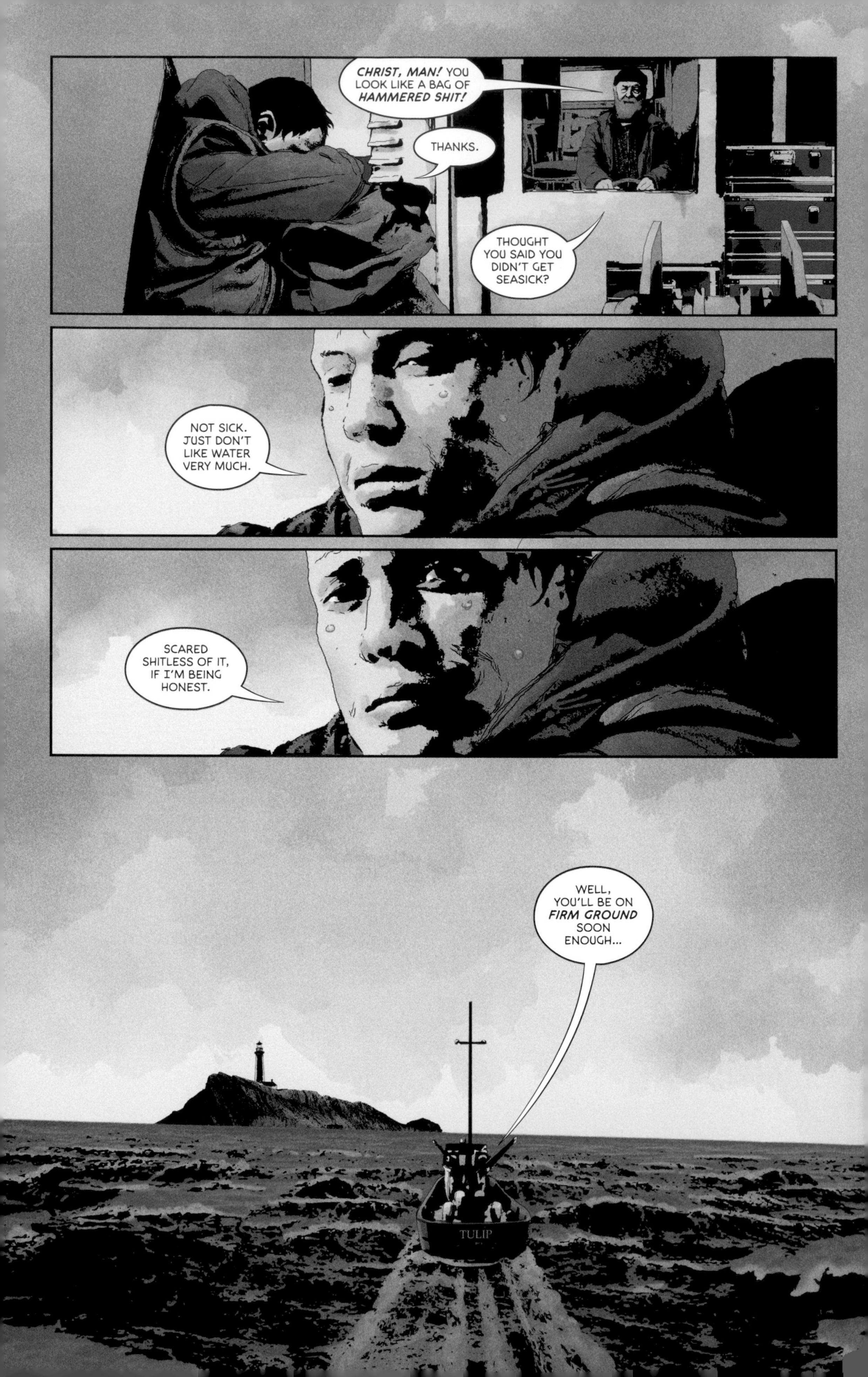
CHRIST, MAN! YOU LOOK LIKE A BAG OF HAMMERED SHIT!
THANKS.
THOUGHT YOU SAID YOU DIDN'T GET SEASICK?
NOT SICK. JUST DON'T LIKE WATER VERY MUCH.
SCARED SHITLESS OF IT, IF I'M BEING HONEST.
WELL, YOU'LL BE ON FIRM GROUND SOON ENOUGH...
TULIP

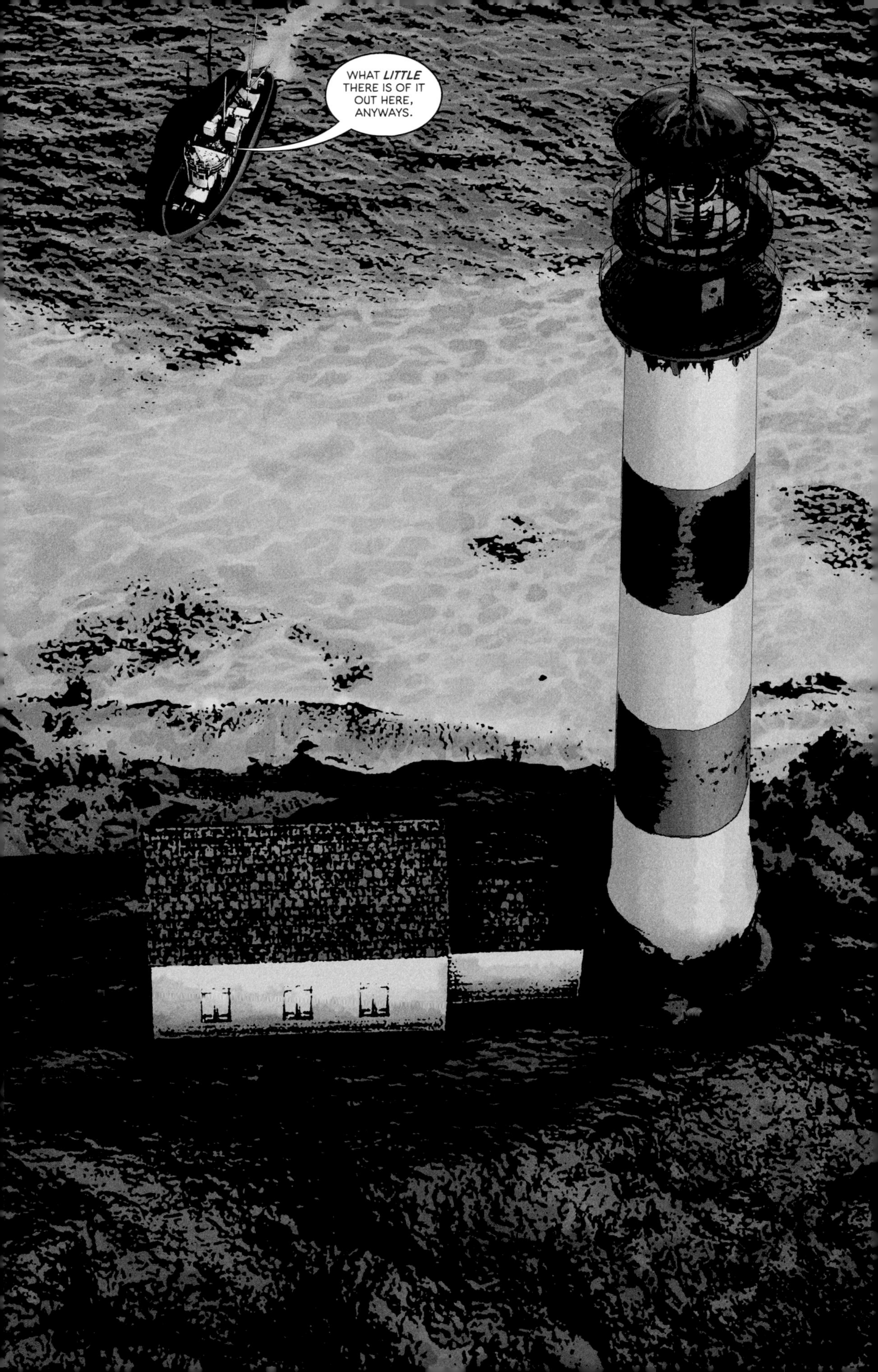
WHAT *LITTLE* THERE IS OF IT OUT HERE, ANYWAYS.

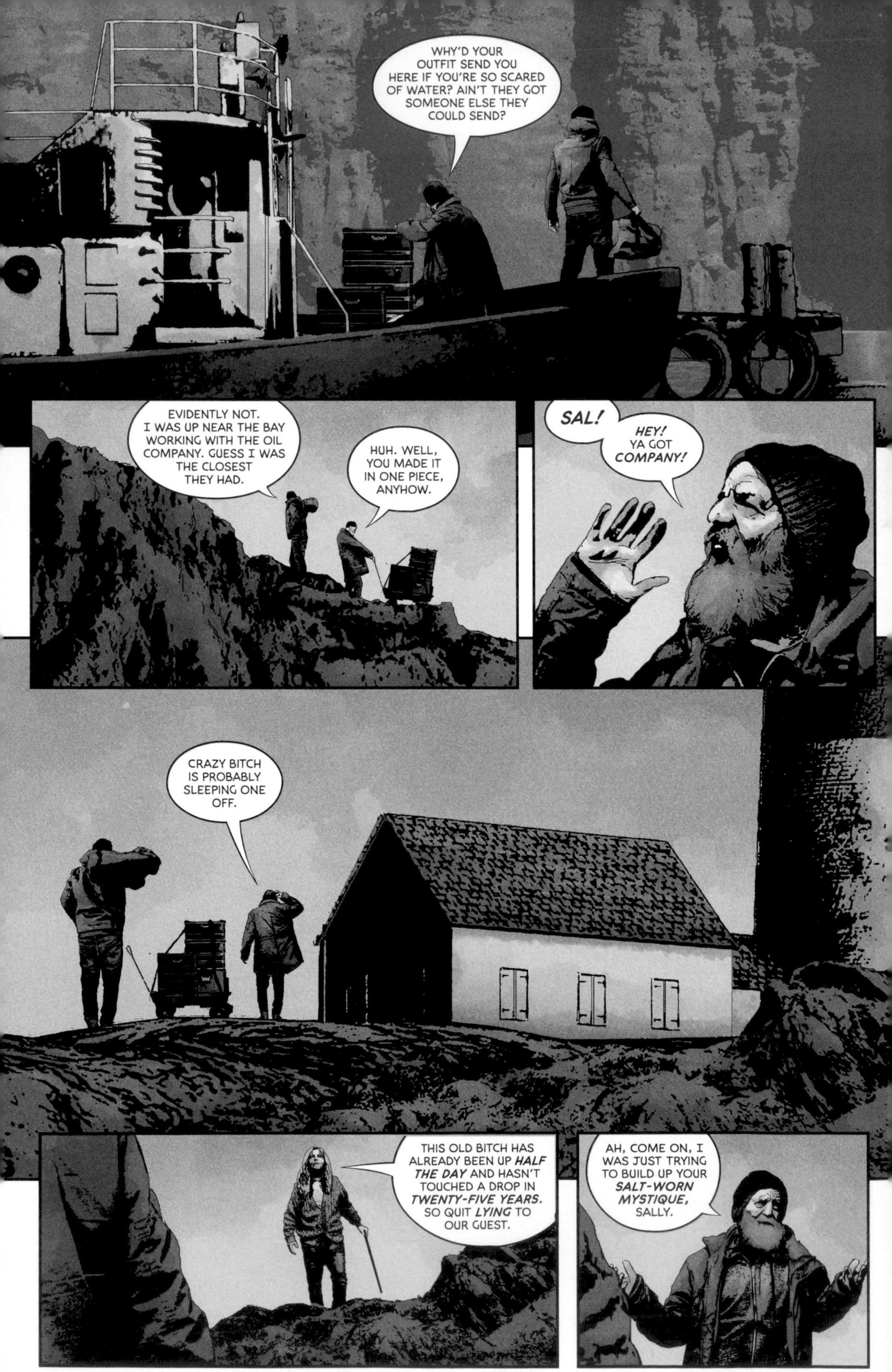
WHY'D YOUR OUTFIT SEND YOU HERE IF YOU'RE SO SCARED OF WATER? AIN'T THEY GOT SOMEONE ELSE THEY COULD SEND?
EVIDENTLY NOT. I WAS UP NEAR THE BAY WORKING WITH THE OIL COMPANY. GUESS I WAS THE CLOSEST THEY HAD.
HUH. WELL, YOU MADE IT IN ONE PIECE, ANYHOW.
SAL!
HEY! YA GOT COMPANY!
CRAZY BITCH IS PROBABLY SLEEPING ONE OFF.
THIS OLD BITCH HAS ALREADY BEEN UP HALF THE DAY AND HASN'T TOUCHED A DROP IN TWENTY-FIVE YEARS. SO QUIT LYING TO OUR GUEST.
AH, COME ON, I WAS JUST TRYING TO BUILD UP YOUR SALT-WORN MYSTIQUE, SALLY.

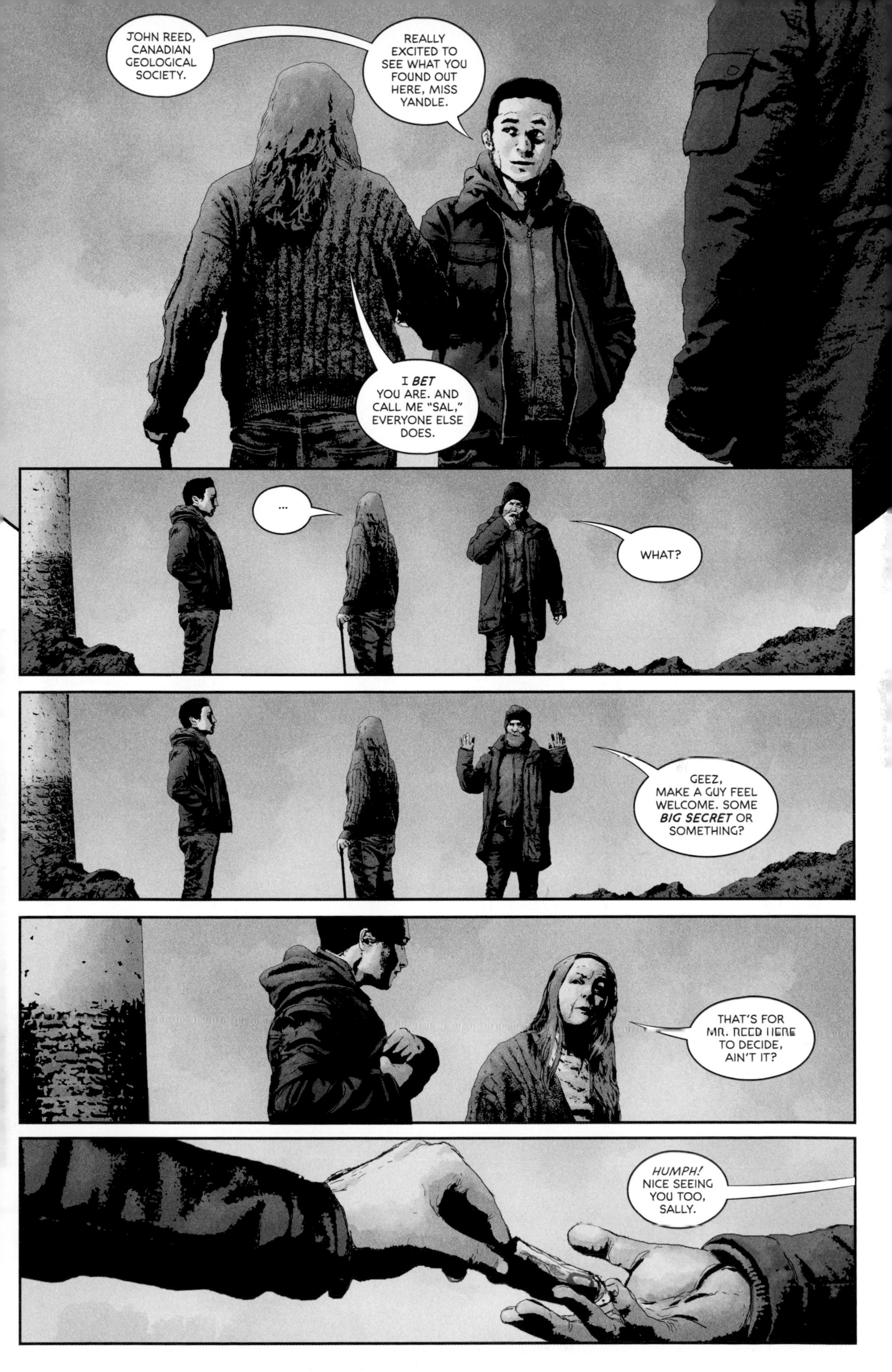
JOHN REED, CANADIAN GEOLOGICAL SOCIETY.
REALLY EXCITED TO SEE WHAT YOU FOUND OUT HERE, MISS YANDLE.
I ***BET*** YOU ARE. AND CALL ME "SAL," EVERYONE ELSE DOES.
...
WHAT?
GEEZ, MAKE A GUY FEEL WELCOME. SOME ***BIG SECRET*** OR SOMETHING?
THAT'S FOR MR. REED HERE TO DECIDE, AIN'T IT?
HUMPH! NICE SEEING YOU TOO, SALLY.

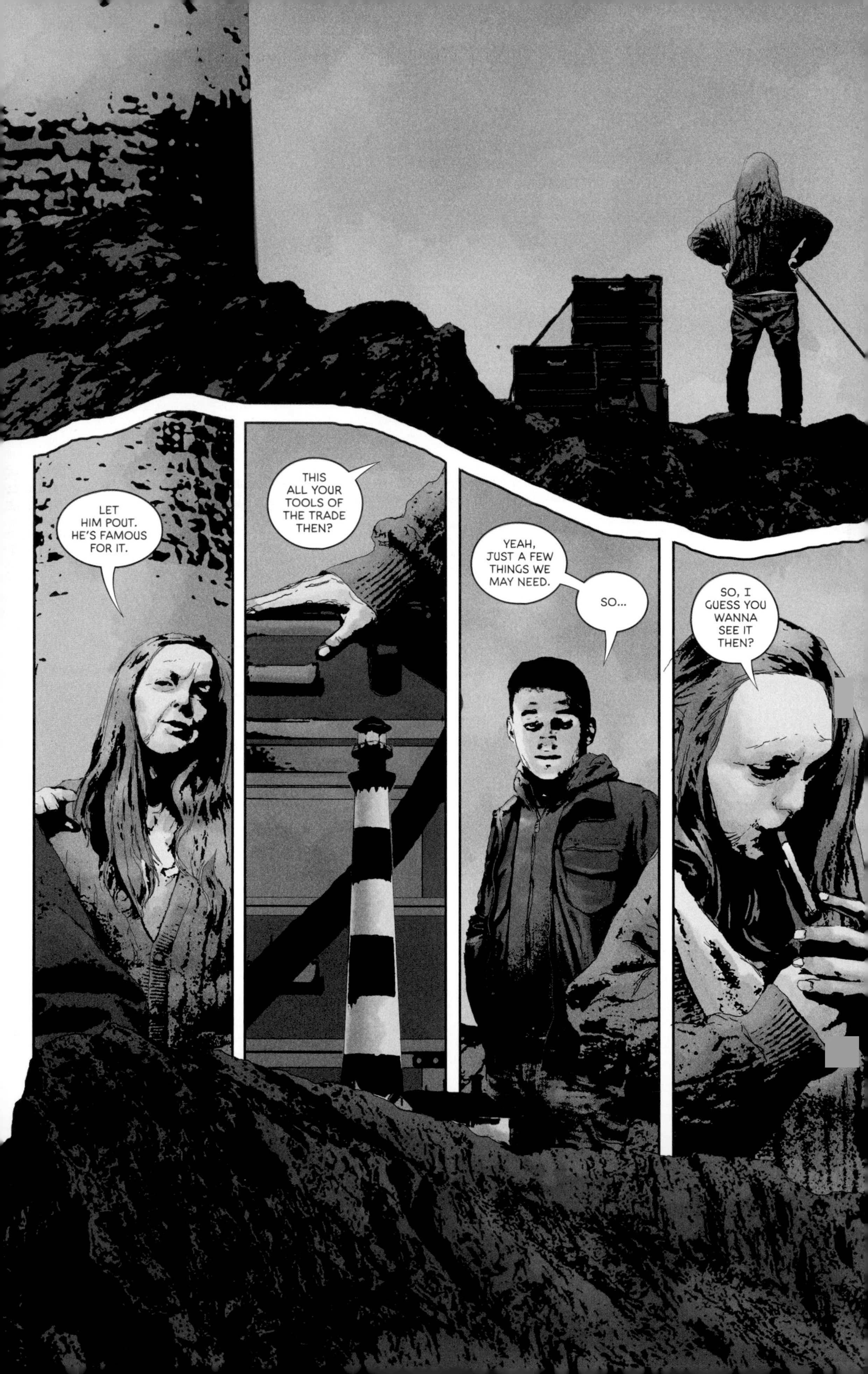
LET HIM POUT. HE'S FAMOUS FOR IT.
THIS ALL YOUR TOOLS OF THE TRADE THEN?
YEAH, JUST A FEW THINGS WE MAY NEED.
SO...
SO, I GUESS YOU WANNA SEE IT THEN?

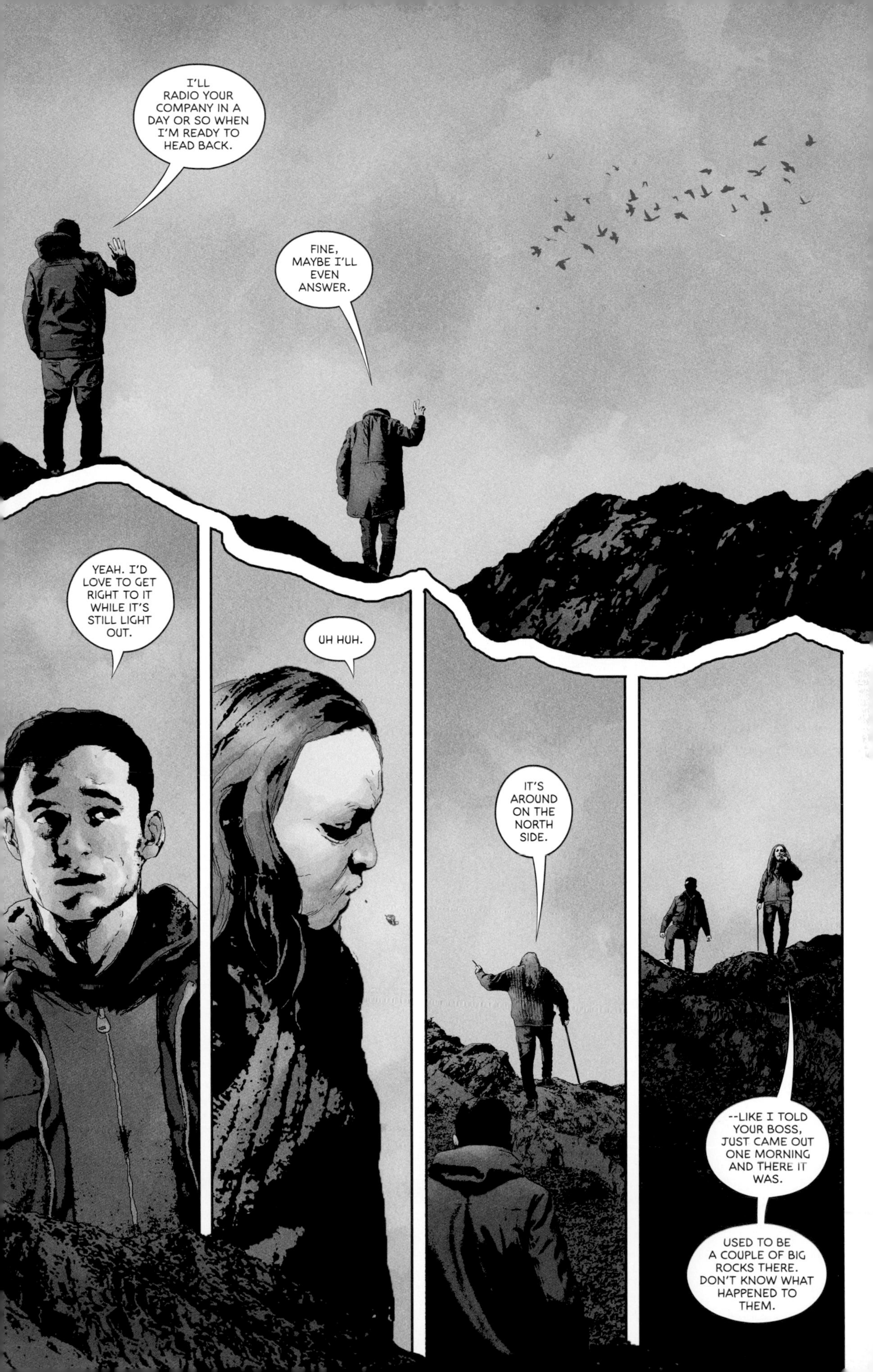
I'LL RADIO YOUR COMPANY IN A DAY OR SO WHEN I'M READY TO HEAD BACK.
FINE, MAYBE I'LL EVEN ANSWER.
YEAH. I'D LOVE TO GET RIGHT TO IT WHILE IT'S STILL LIGHT OUT.
UH HUH.
IT'S AROUND ON THE NORTH SIDE.
--LIKE I TOLD YOUR BOSS, JUST CAME OUT ONE MORNING AND THERE IT WAS.
USED TO BE A COUPLE OF BIG ROCKS THERE. DON'T KNOW WHAT HAPPENED TO THEM.

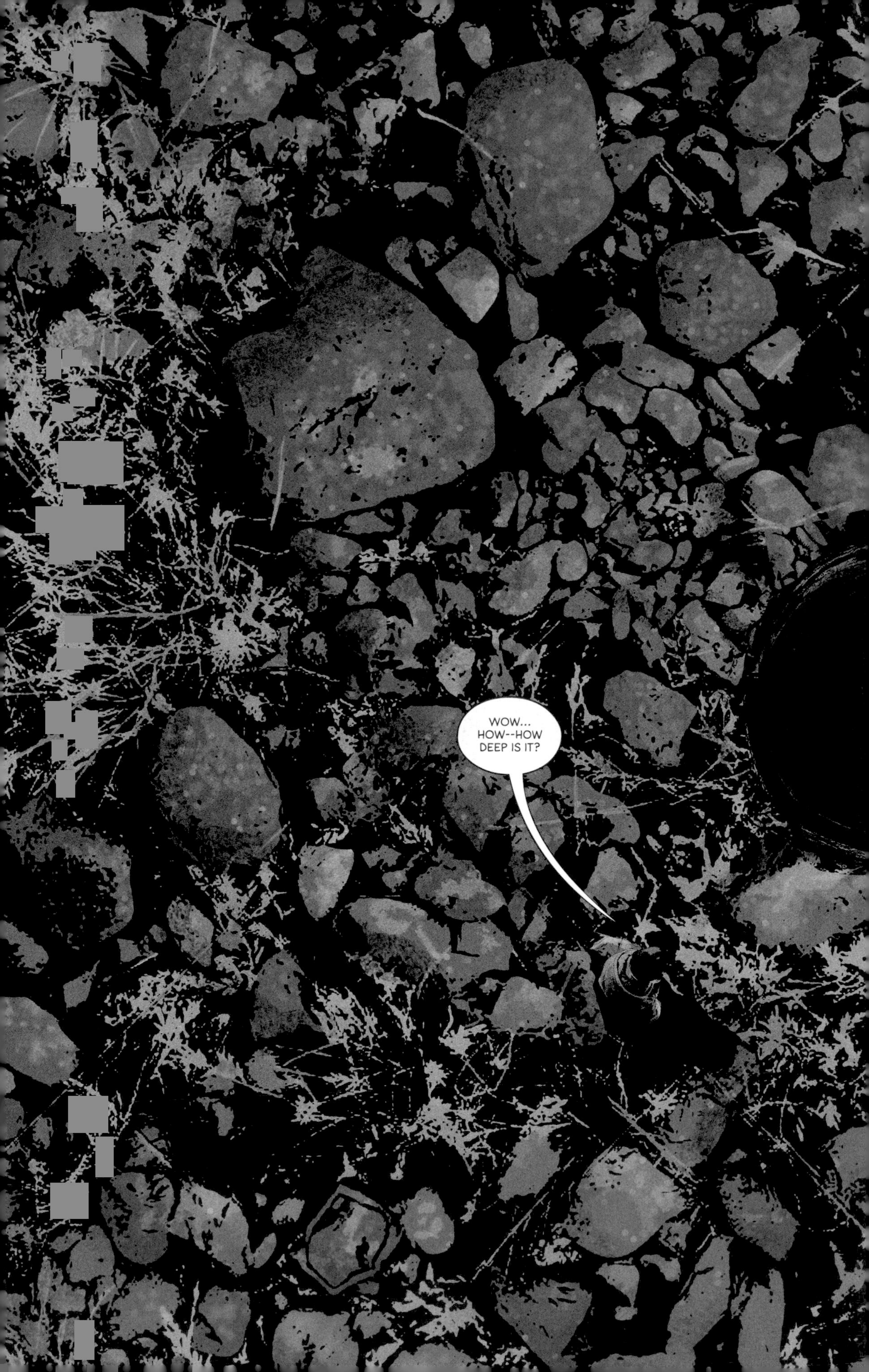
WOW... HOW--HOW DEEP IS IT?

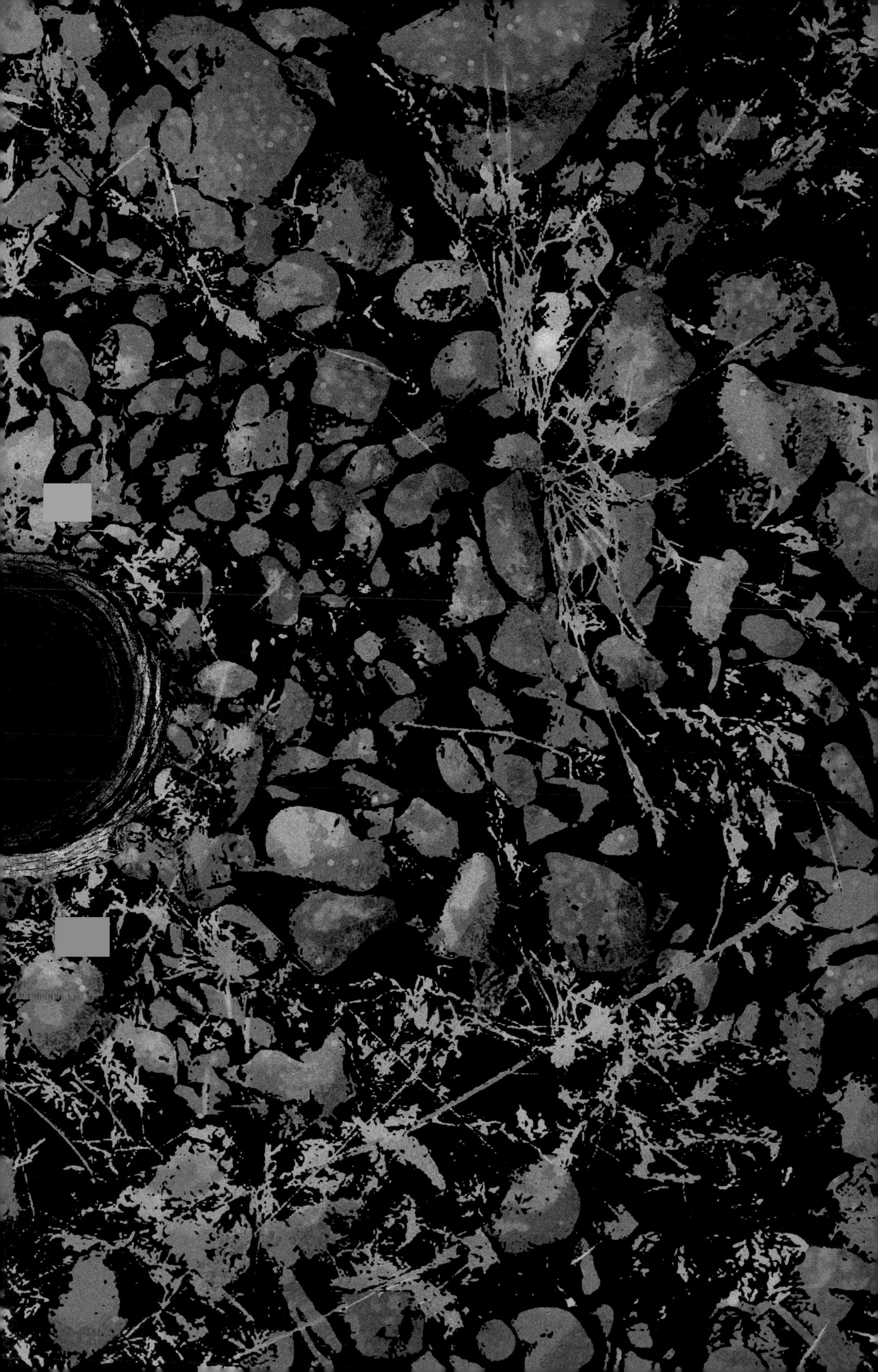

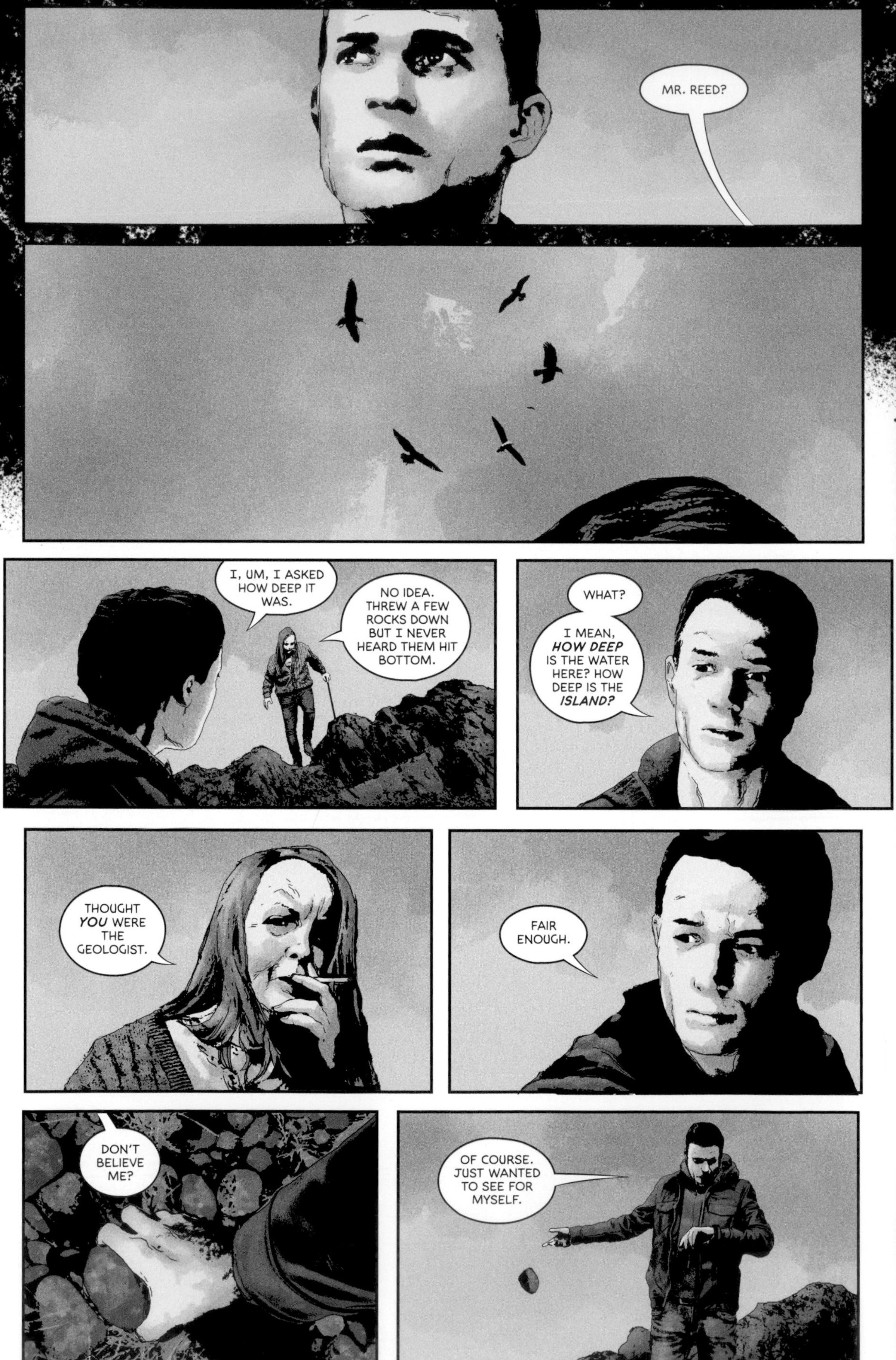
MR. REED?
I, UM, I ASKED HOW DEEP IT WAS.
NO IDEA. THREW A FEW ROCKS DOWN BUT I NEVER HEARD THEM HIT BOTTOM.
WHAT?
I MEAN, HOW DEEP IS THE WATER HERE? HOW DEEP IS THE ISLAND?
THOUGHT YOU WERE THE GEOLOGIST.
FAIR ENOUGH.
DON'T BELIEVE ME?
OF COURSE. JUST WANTED TO SEE FOR MYSELF.

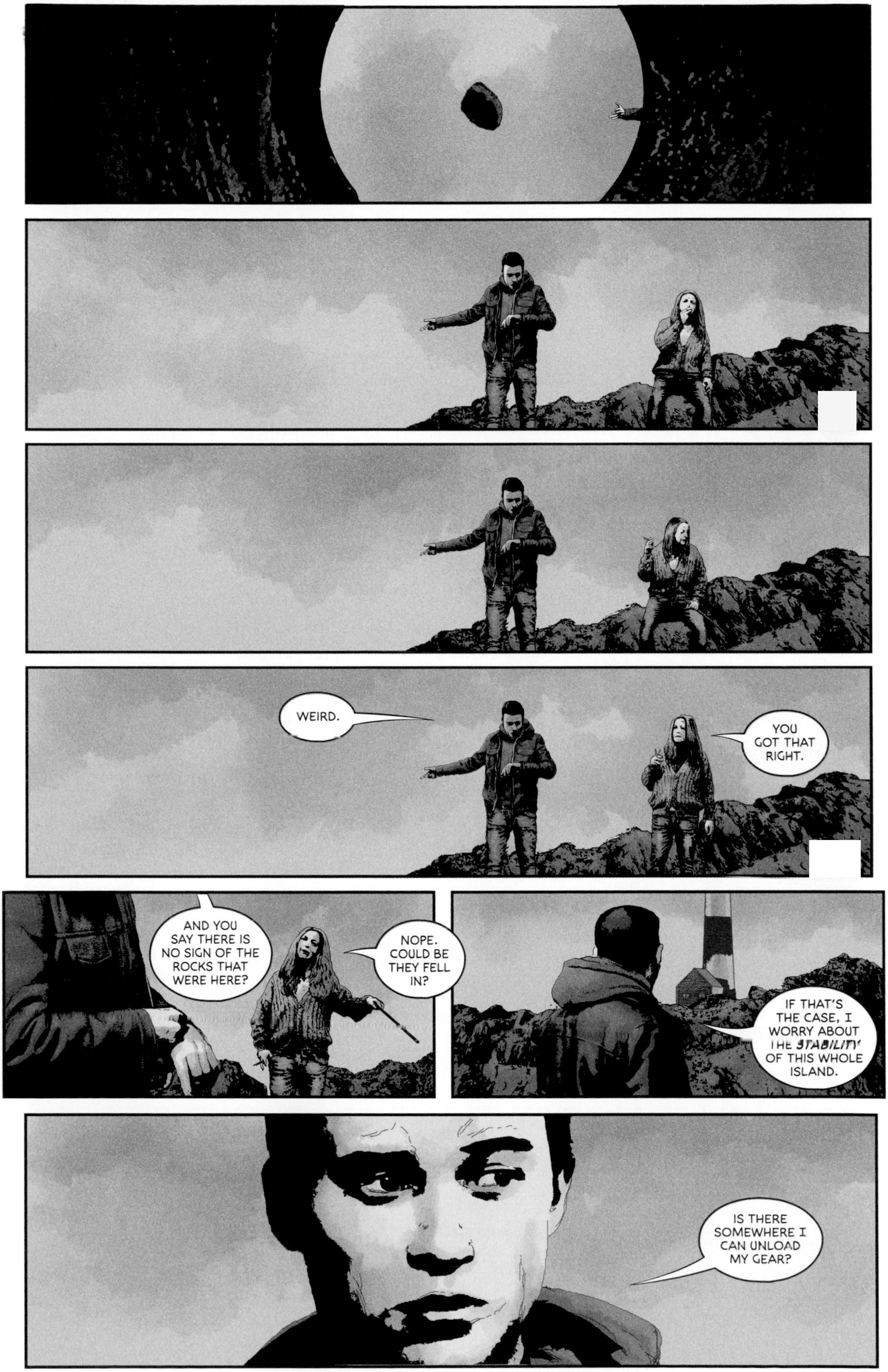
WEIRD.
YOU GOT THAT RIGHT.
AND YOU SAY THERE IS NO SIGN OF THE ROCKS THAT WERE HERE?
NOPE. COULD BE THEY FELL IN?
IF THAT'S THE CASE, I WORRY ABOUT THE STABILITY OF THIS WHOLE ISLAND.
IS THERE SOMEWHERE I CAN UNLOAD MY GEAR?

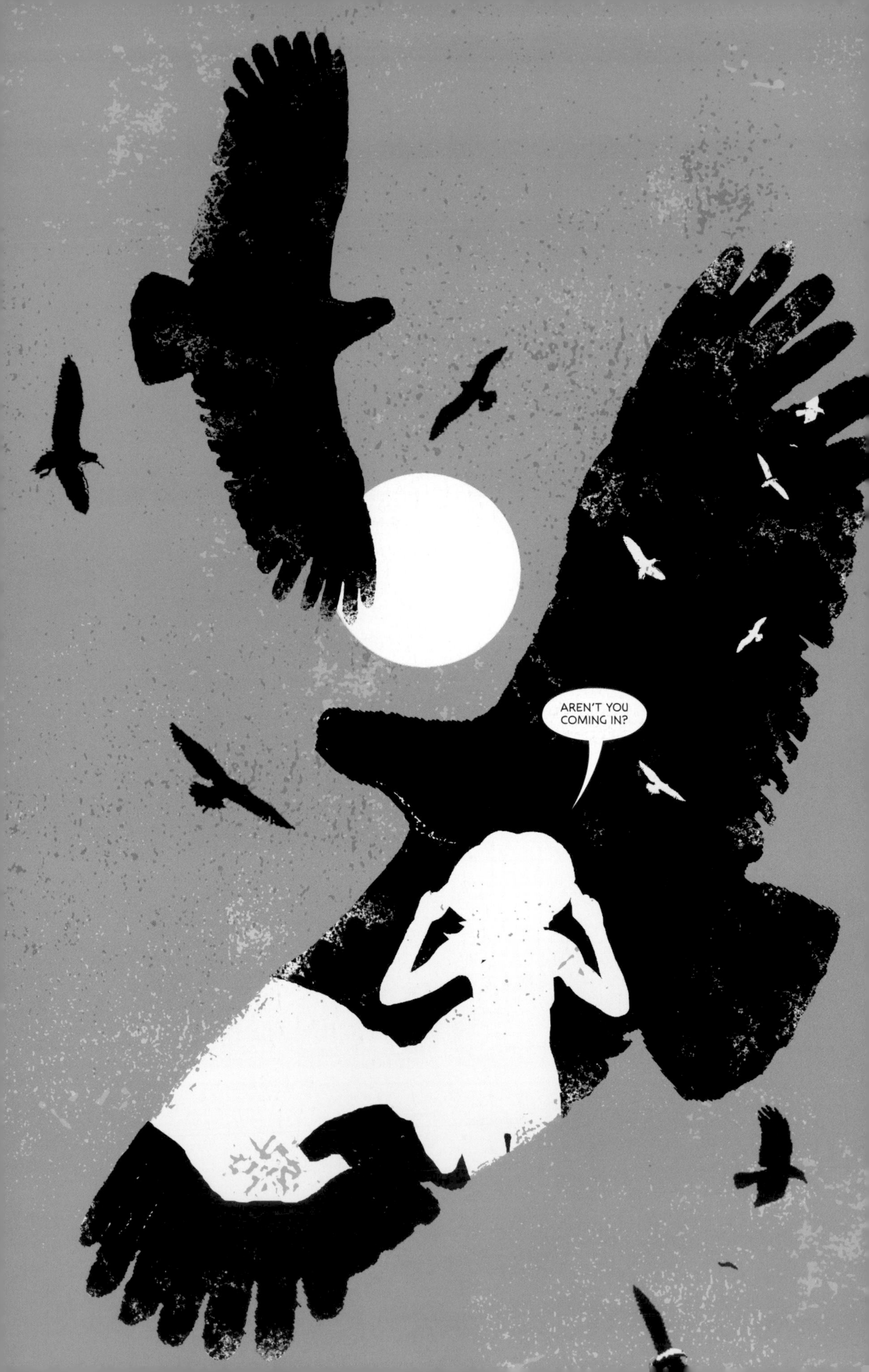
AREN'T YOU COMING IN?

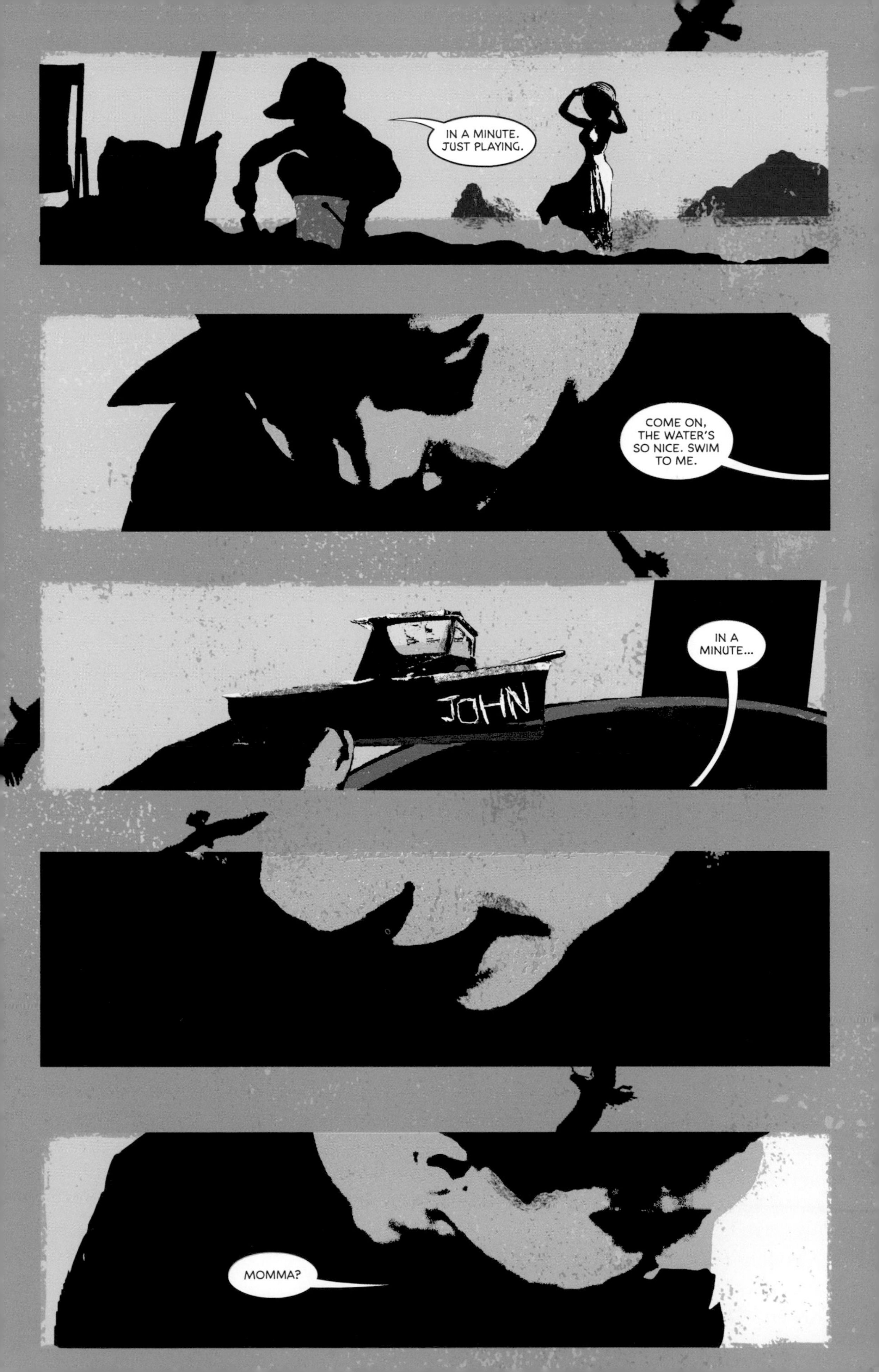
IN A MINUTE. JUST PLAYING.
COME ON, THE WATER'S SO NICE. SWIM TO ME.
JOHN
IN A MINUTE...
MOMMA?

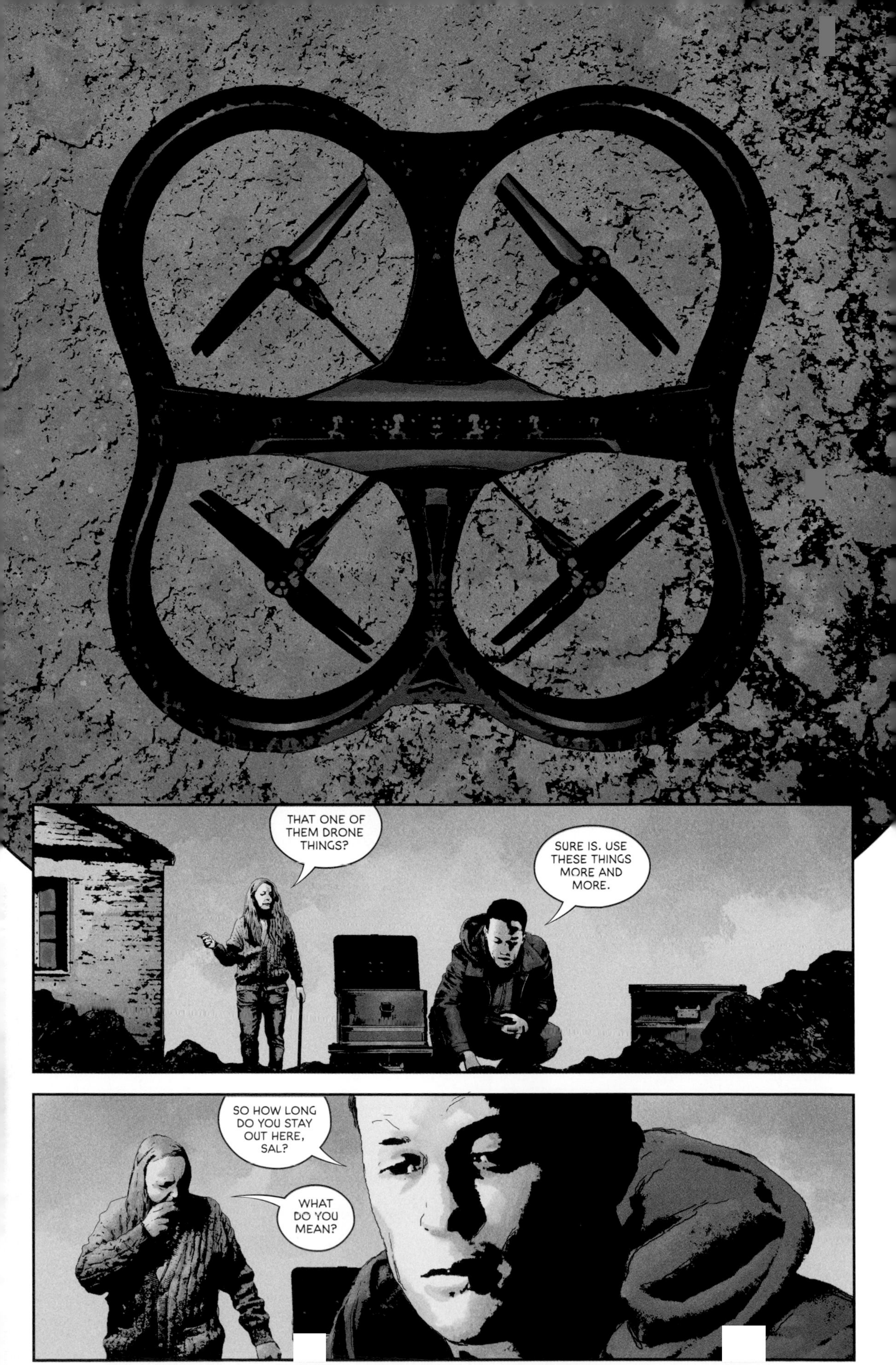
THAT ONE OF THEM DRONE THINGS?
SURE IS. USE THESE THINGS MORE AND MORE.
SO HOW LONG DO YOU STAY OUT HERE, SAL?
WHAT DO YOU MEAN?

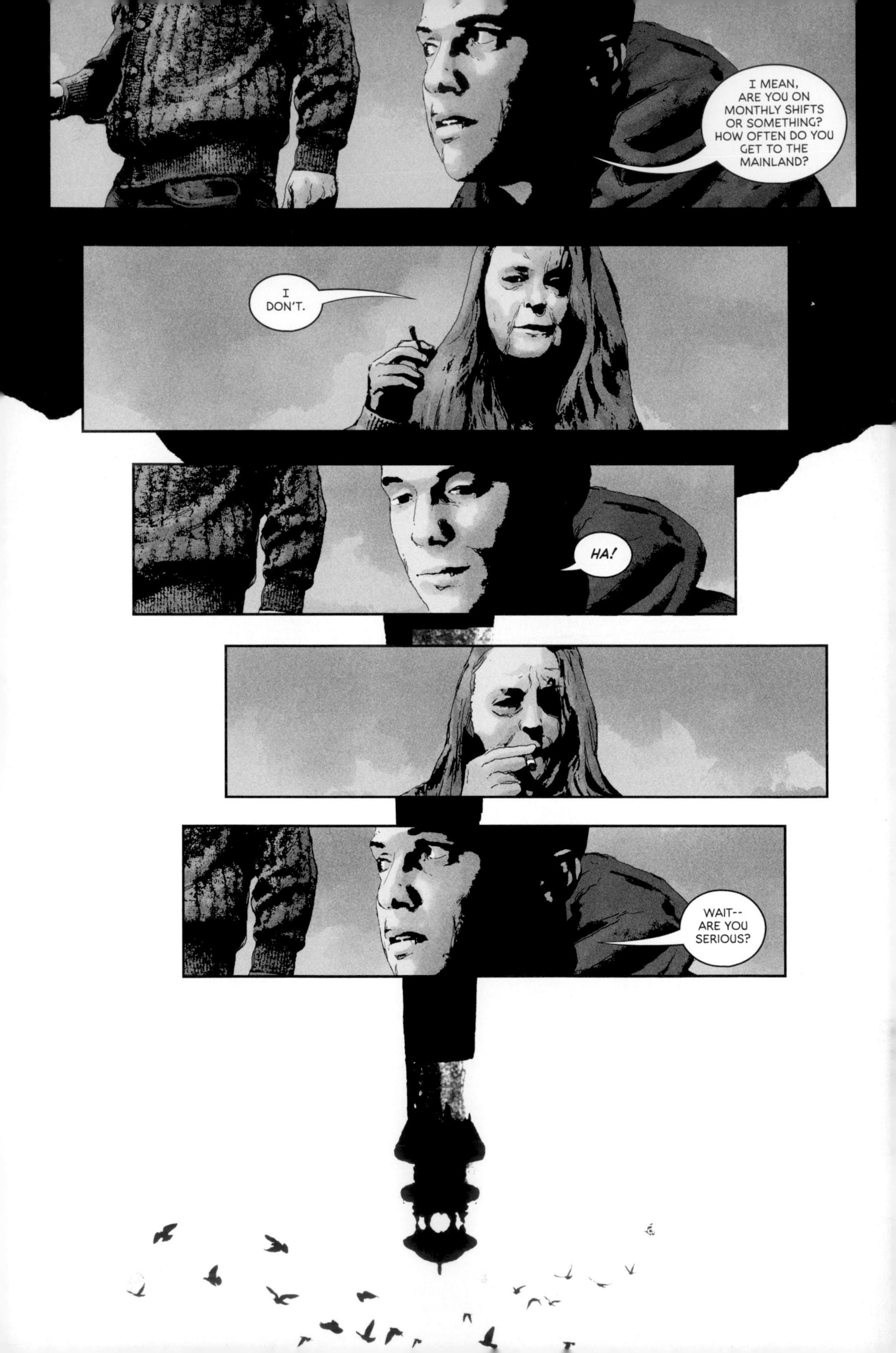
I MEAN, ARE YOU ON MONTHLY SHIFTS OR SOMETHING? HOW OFTEN DO YOU GET TO THE MAINLAND?
I DON'T.
HA!
WAIT-- ARE YOU SERIOUS?

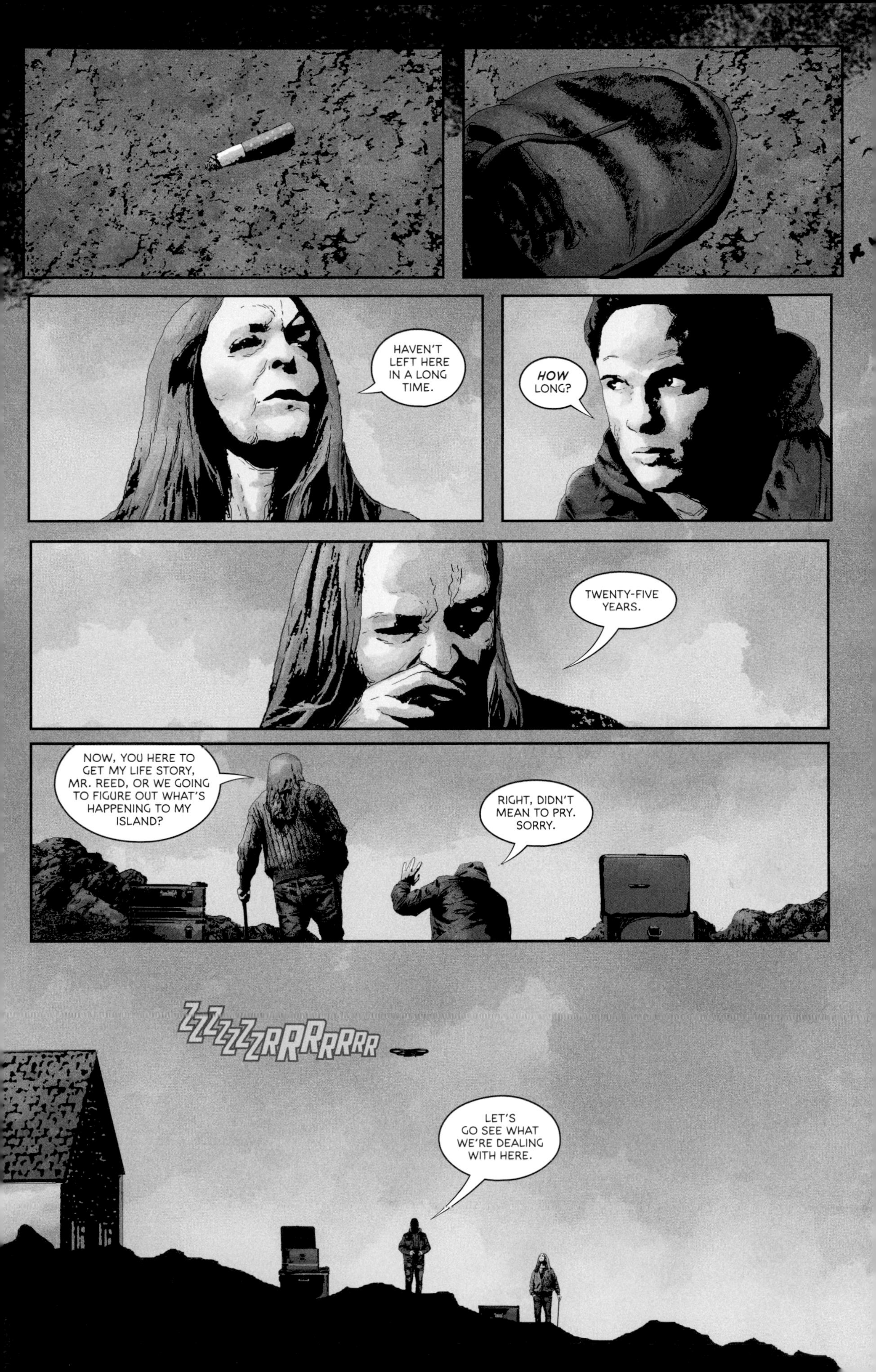
HAVEN'T LEFT HERE IN A LONG TIME.
HOW LONG?
TWENTY-FIVE YEARS.
NOW, YOU HERE TO GET MY LIFE STORY, MR. REED, OR WE GOING TO FIGURE OUT WHAT'S HAPPENING TO MY ISLAND?
RIGHT, DIDN'T MEAN TO PRY. SORRY.
ZZZZZZRRRRRRR
LET'S GO SEE WHAT WE'RE DEALING WITH HERE.

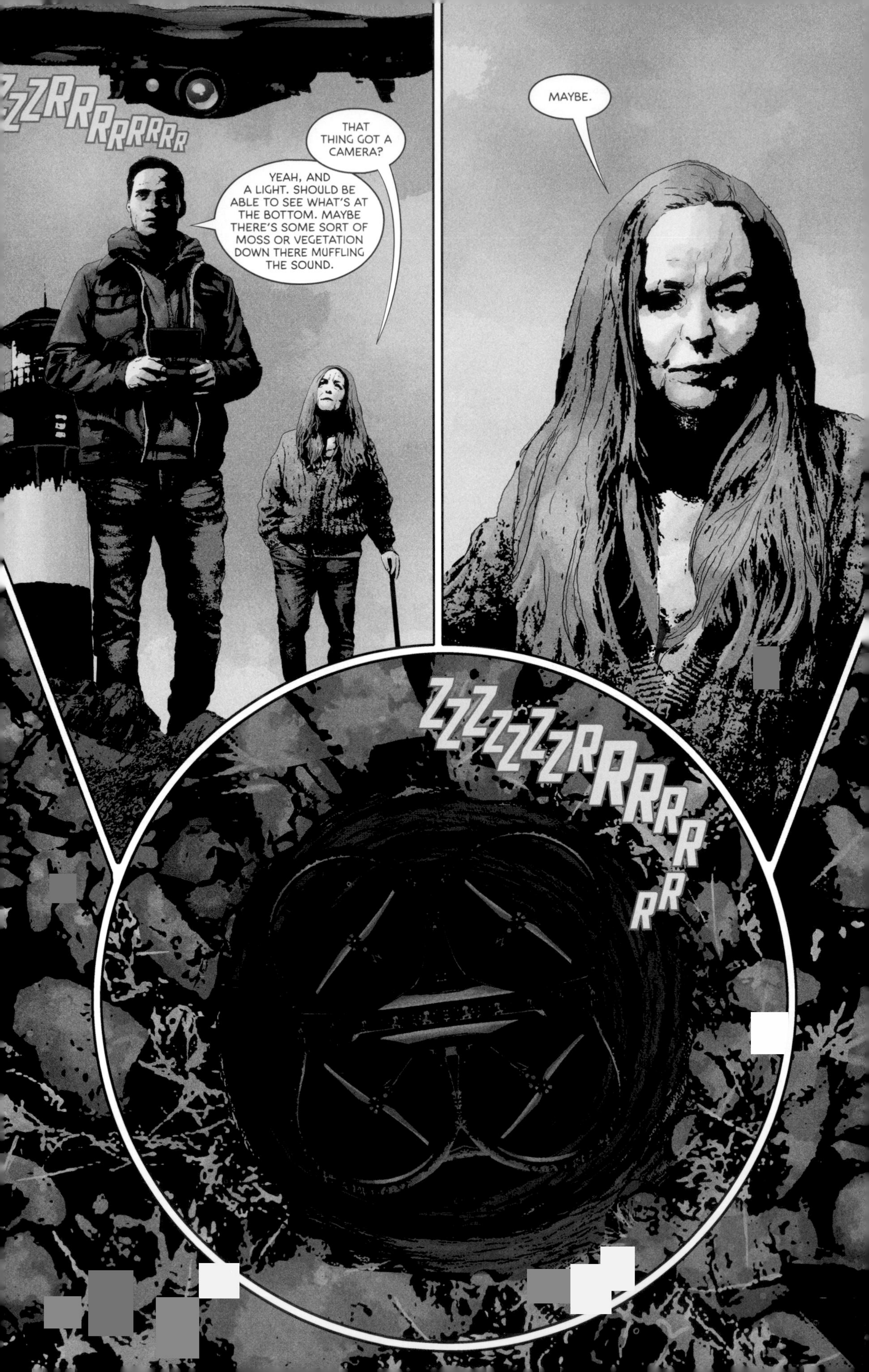
ZZZRRRRRRRR
THAT THING GOT A CAMERA?
YEAH, AND A LIGHT. SHOULD BE ABLE TO SEE WHAT'S AT THE BOTTOM. MAYBE THERE'S SOME SORT OF MOSS OR VEGETATION DOWN THERE MUFFLING THE SOUND.
MAYBE.
ZZZZZZRRRRRRRR

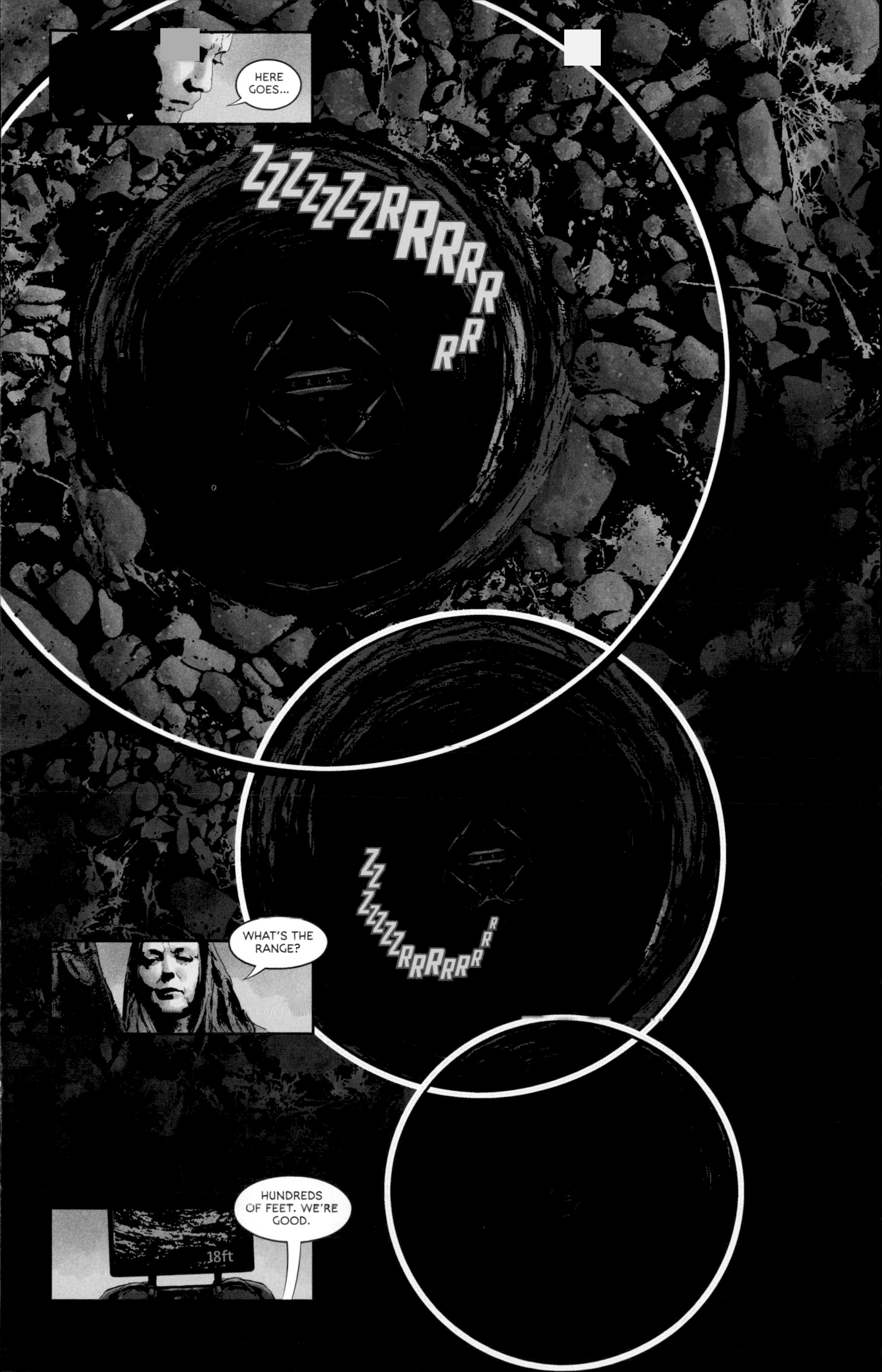
HERE GOES...
ZZZZZZZRRRRRRRR
ZZZZZZZZRRRRRRRR
WHAT'S THE RANGE?
HUNDREDS OF FEET. WE'RE GOOD.
18ft

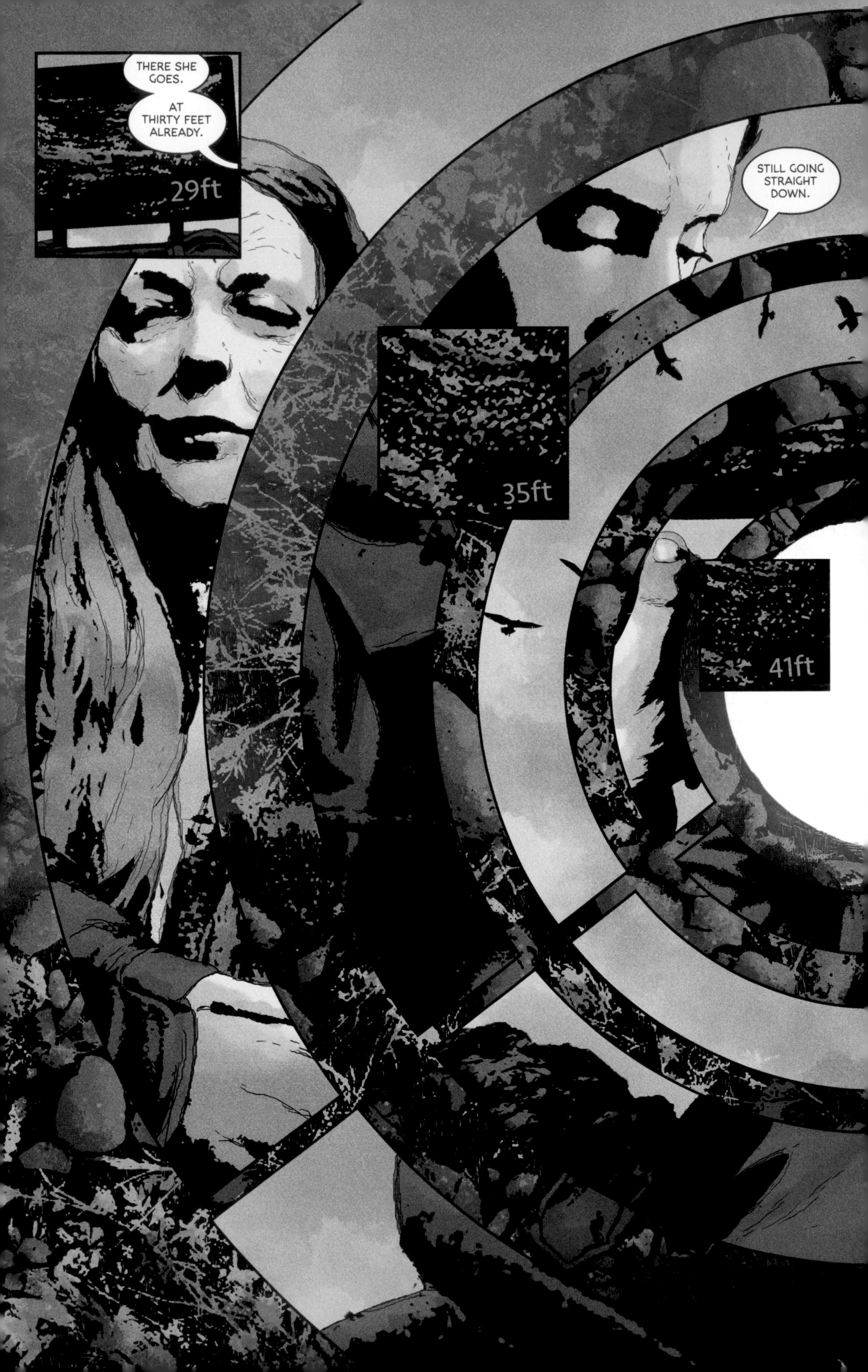
THERE SHE GOES.
AT THIRTY FEET ALREADY.
29ft
STILL GOING STRAIGHT DOWN.
35ft
41ft

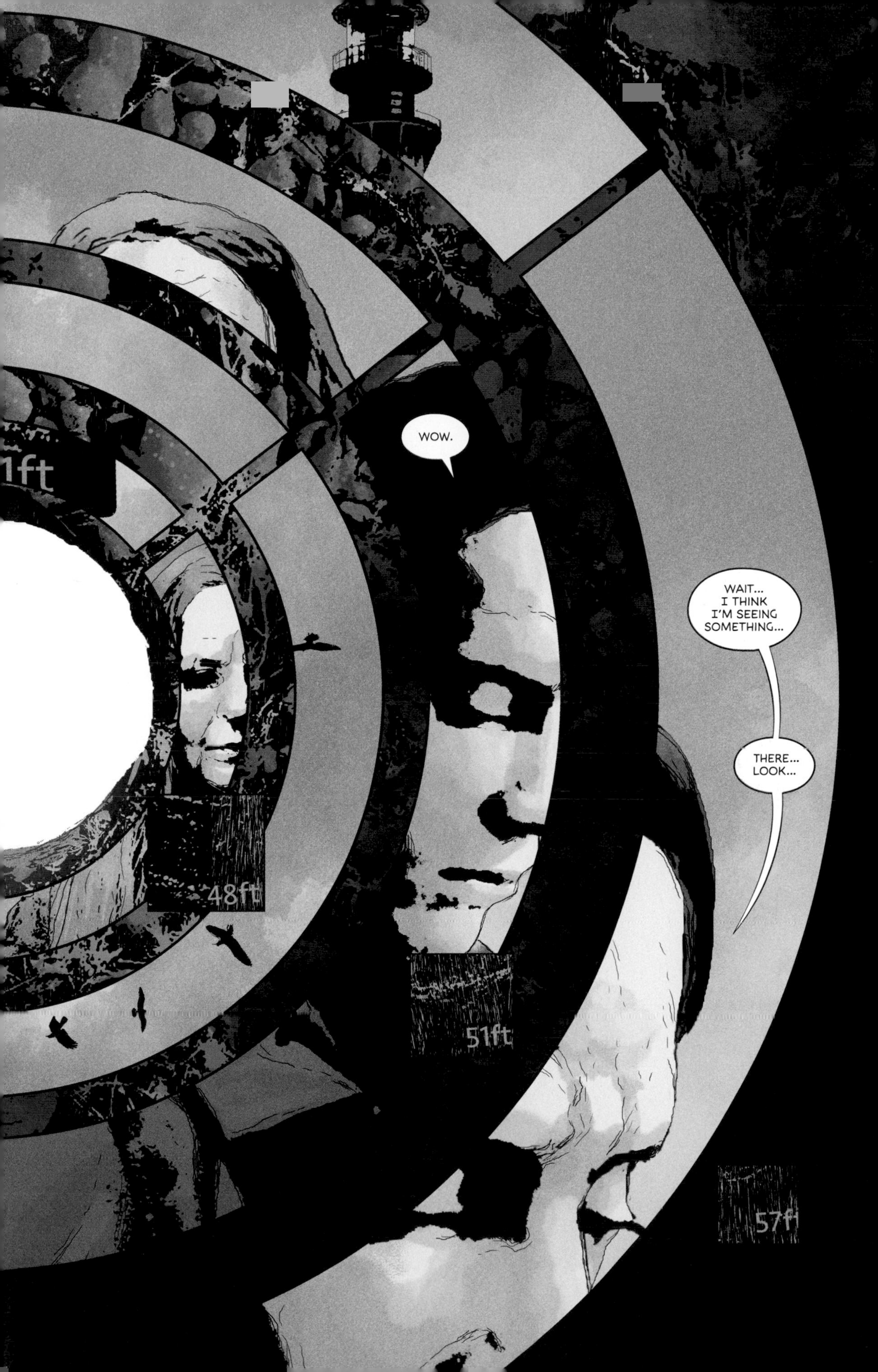
48ft
WOW.
51ft
WAIT... I THINK I'M SEEING SOMETHING...
THERE... LOOK...

60ft
--WHAT THE FUCK?!

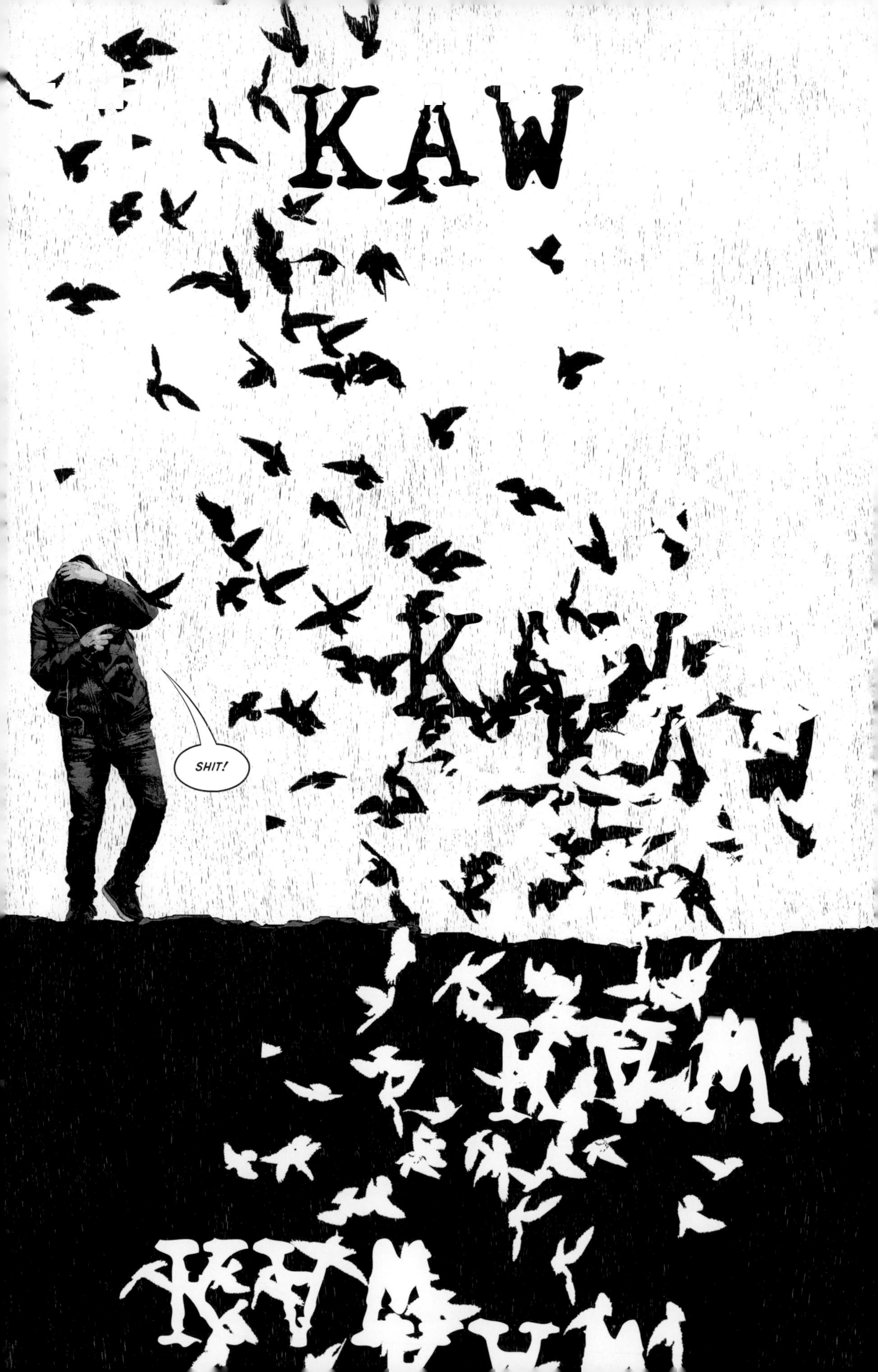
KAW
KAW
SHIT!

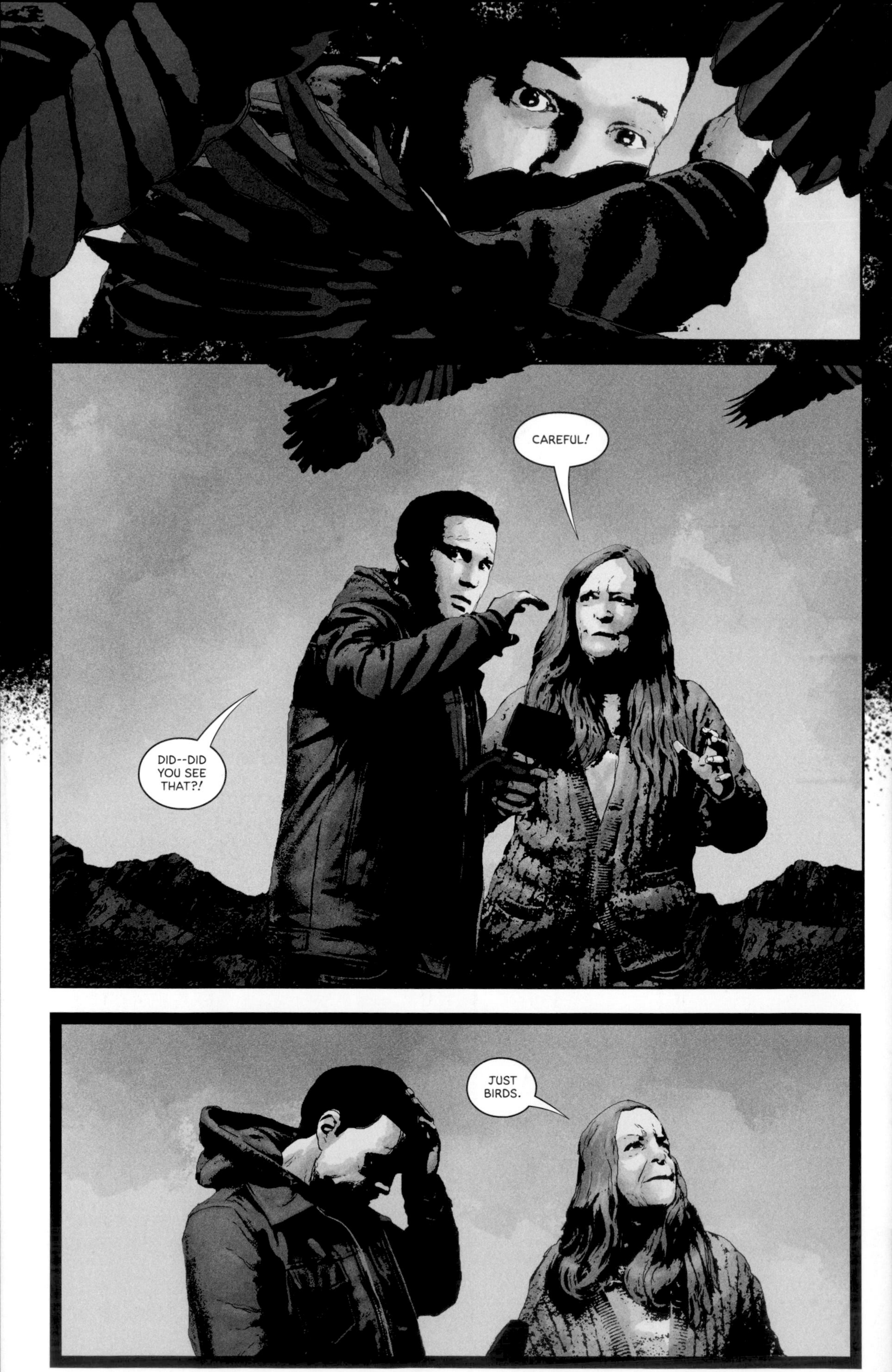
CAREFUL!
DID--DID YOU SEE THAT?!
JUST BIRDS.

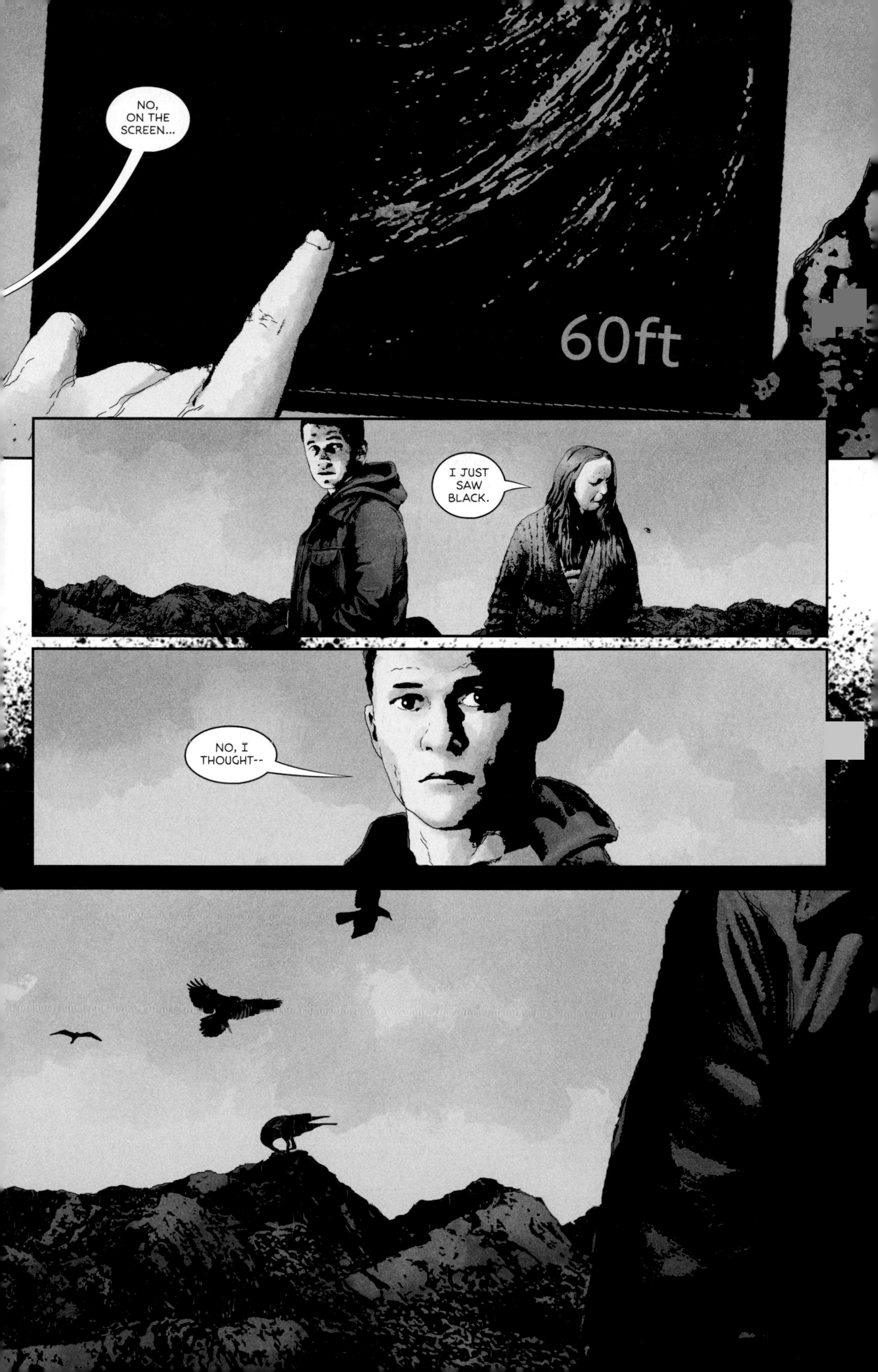
NO, ON THE SCREEN...
60ft
I JUST SAW BLACK.
NO, I THOUGHT--

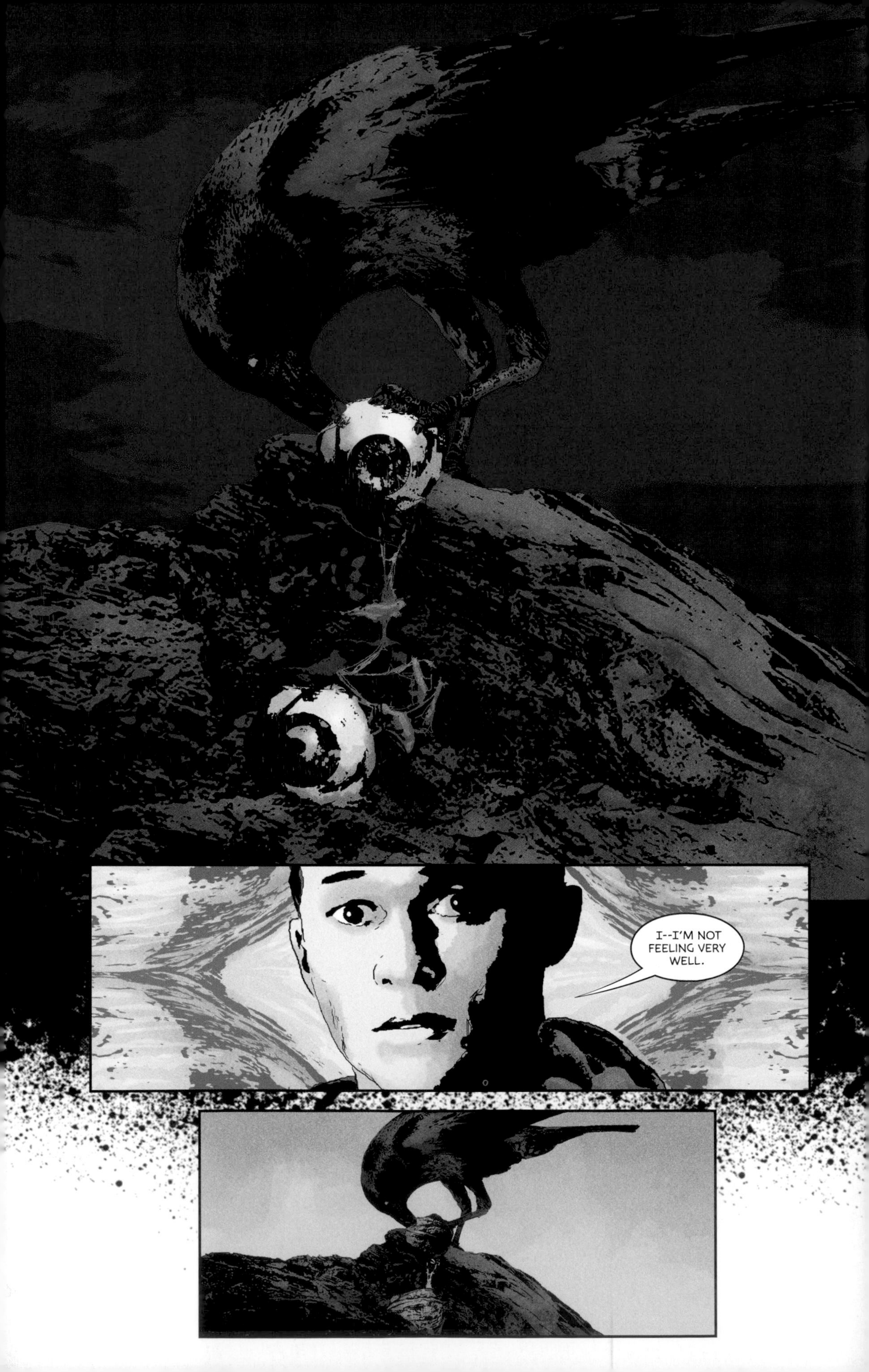
I--I'M NOT FEELING VERY WELL.

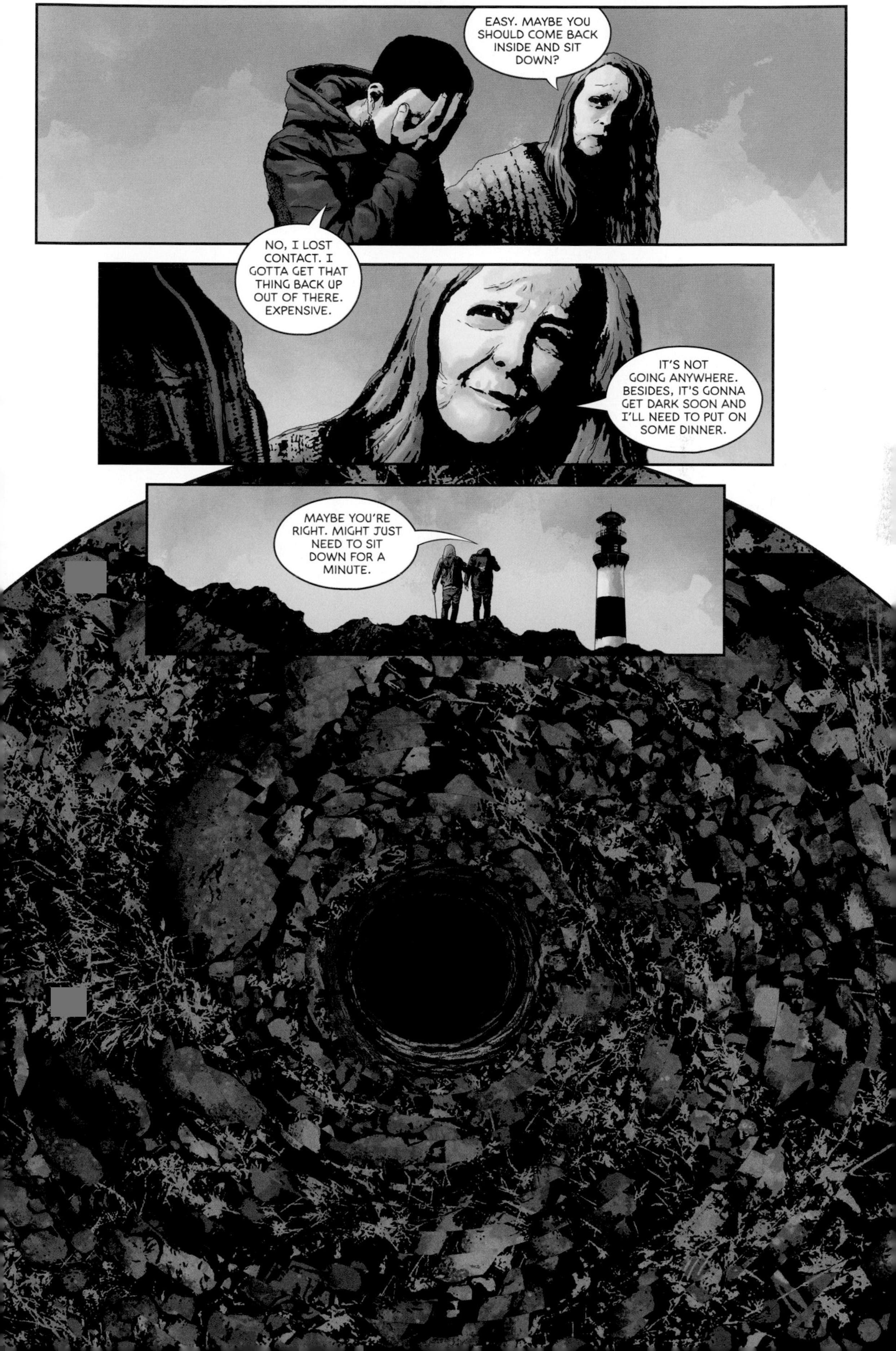
EASY. MAYBE YOU SHOULD COME BACK INSIDE AND SIT DOWN?
NO, I LOST CONTACT. I GOTTA GET THAT THING BACK UP OUT OF THERE. EXPENSIVE.
IT'S NOT GOING ANYWHERE. BESIDES, IT'S GONNA GET DARK SOON AND I'LL NEED TO PUT ON SOME DINNER.
MAYBE YOU'RE RIGHT. MIGHT JUST NEED TO SIT DOWN FOR A MINUTE.

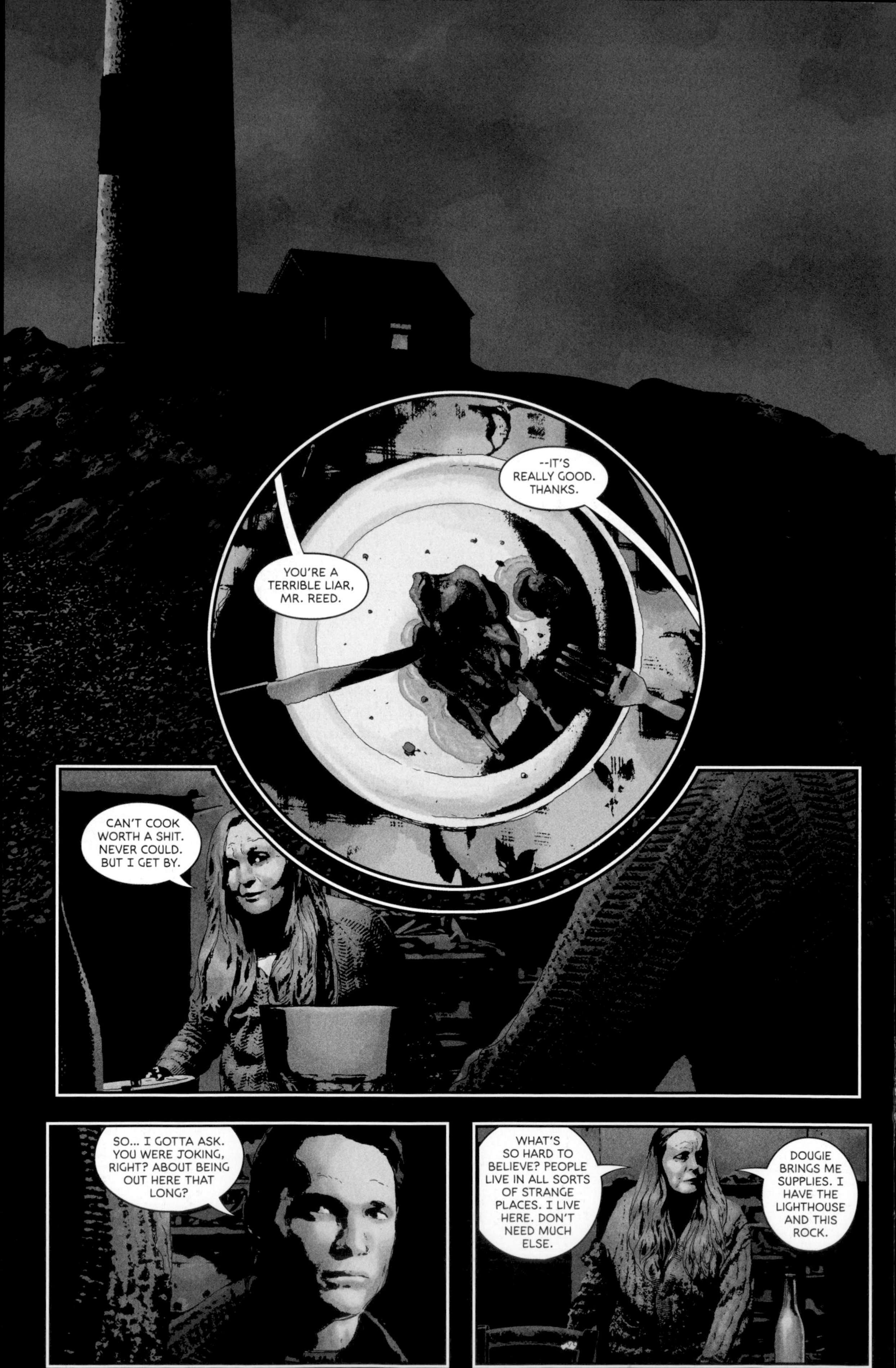
--IT'S REALLY GOOD. THANKS.
YOU'RE A TERRIBLE LIAR, MR. REED.
CAN'T COOK WORTH A SHIT. NEVER COULD. BUT I GET BY.
SO... I GOTTA ASK. YOU WERE JOKING, RIGHT? ABOUT BEING OUT HERE THAT LONG?
WHAT'S SO HARD TO BELIEVE? PEOPLE LIVE IN ALL SORTS OF STRANGE PLACES. I LIVE HERE. DON'T NEED MUCH ELSE.
DOUGIE BRINGS ME SUPPLIES. I HAVE THE LIGHTHOUSE AND THIS ROCK.

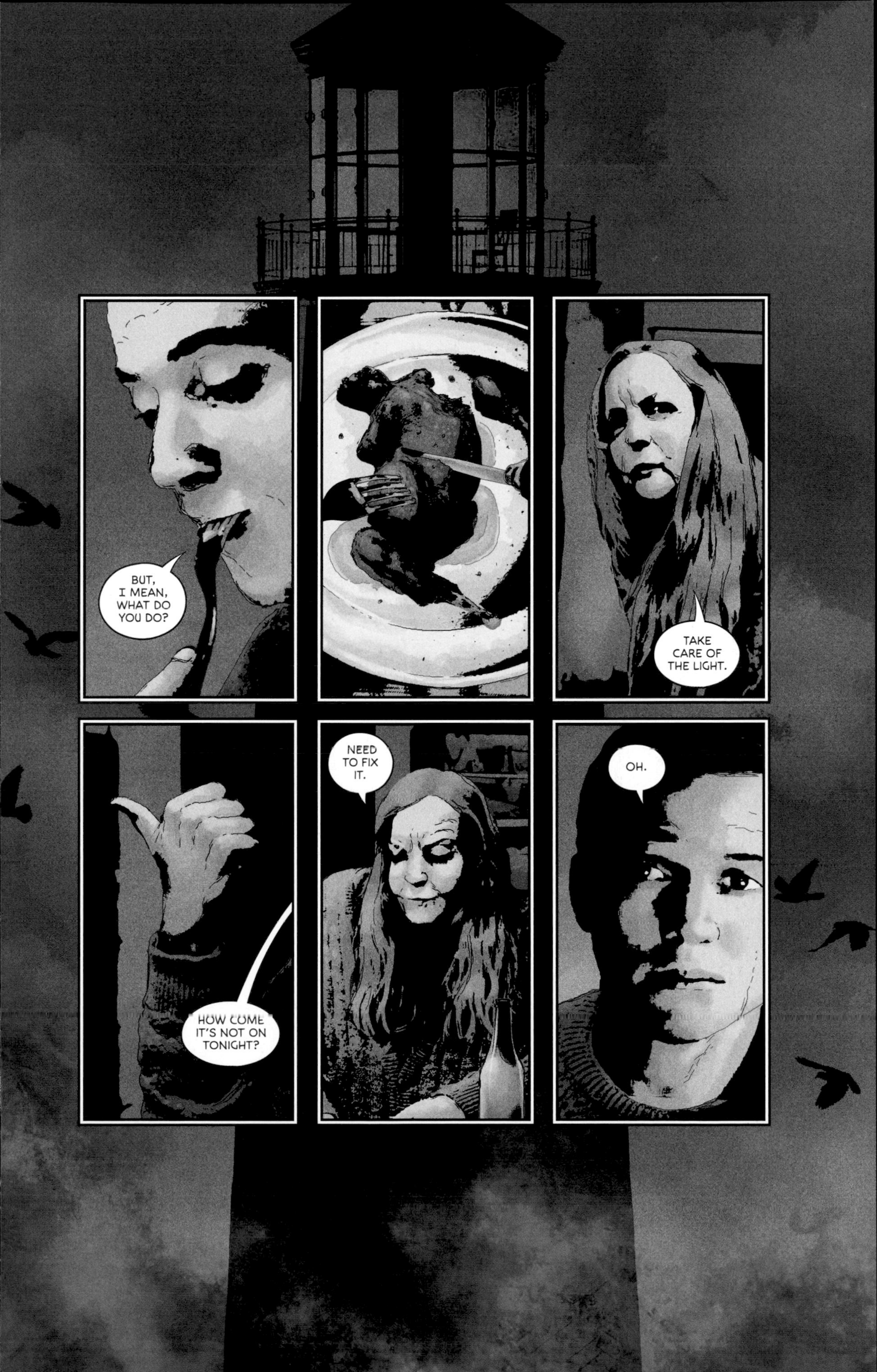
BUT, I MEAN, WHAT DO YOU DO?
TAKE CARE OF THE LIGHT.
HOW COME IT'S NOT ON TONIGHT?
NEED TO FIX IT.
OH.

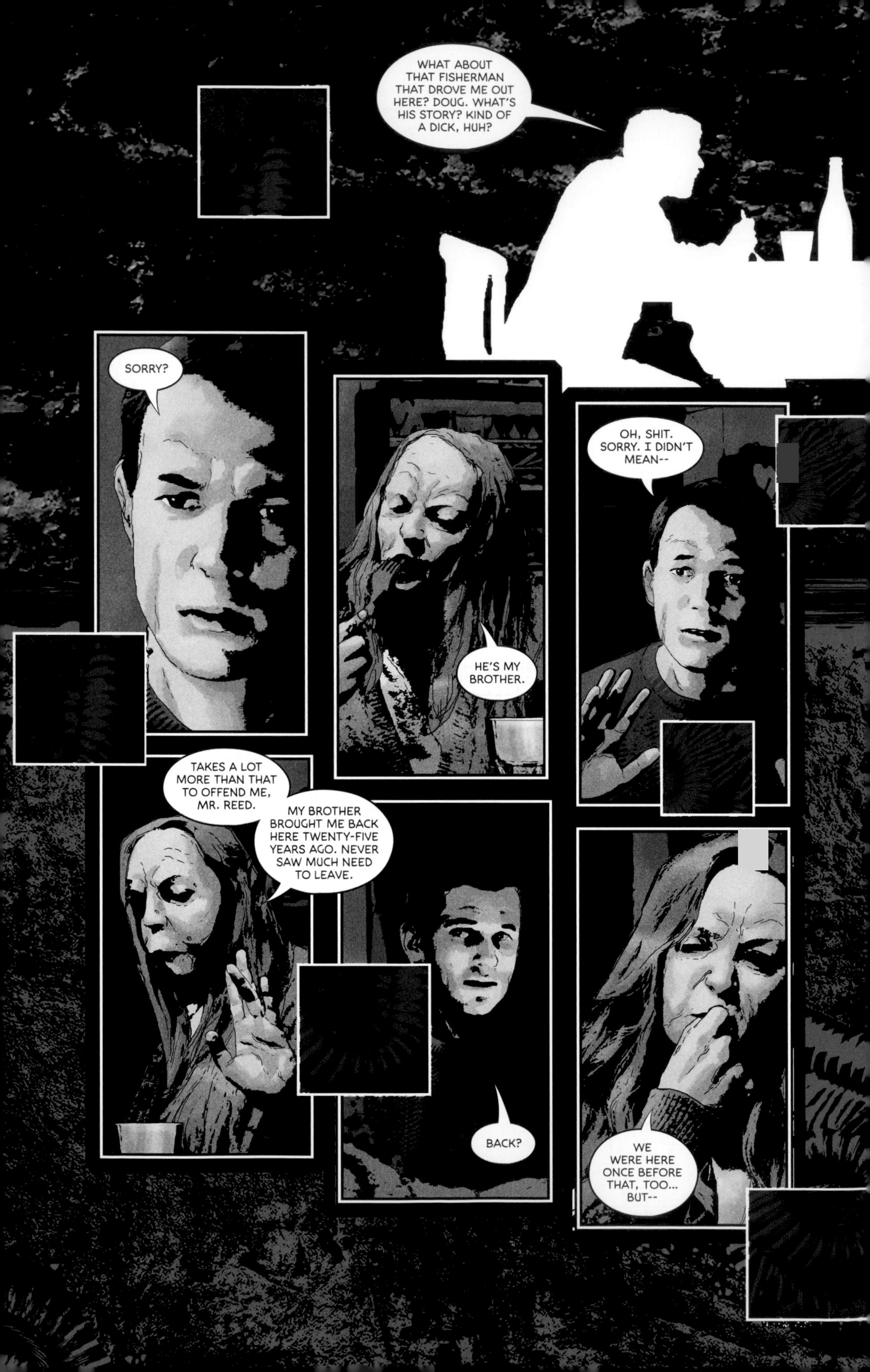
WHAT ABOUT THAT FISHERMAN THAT DROVE ME OUT HERE? DOUG. WHAT'S HIS STORY? KIND OF A DICK, HUH?
SORRY?
HE'S MY BROTHER.
OH, SHIT. SORRY. I DIDN'T MEAN--
TAKES A LOT MORE THAN THAT TO OFFEND ME, MR. REED.
MY BROTHER BROUGHT ME BACK HERE TWENTY-FIVE YEARS AGO. NEVER SAW MUCH NEED TO LEAVE.
BACK?
WE WERE HERE ONCE BEFORE THAT, TOO... BUT--

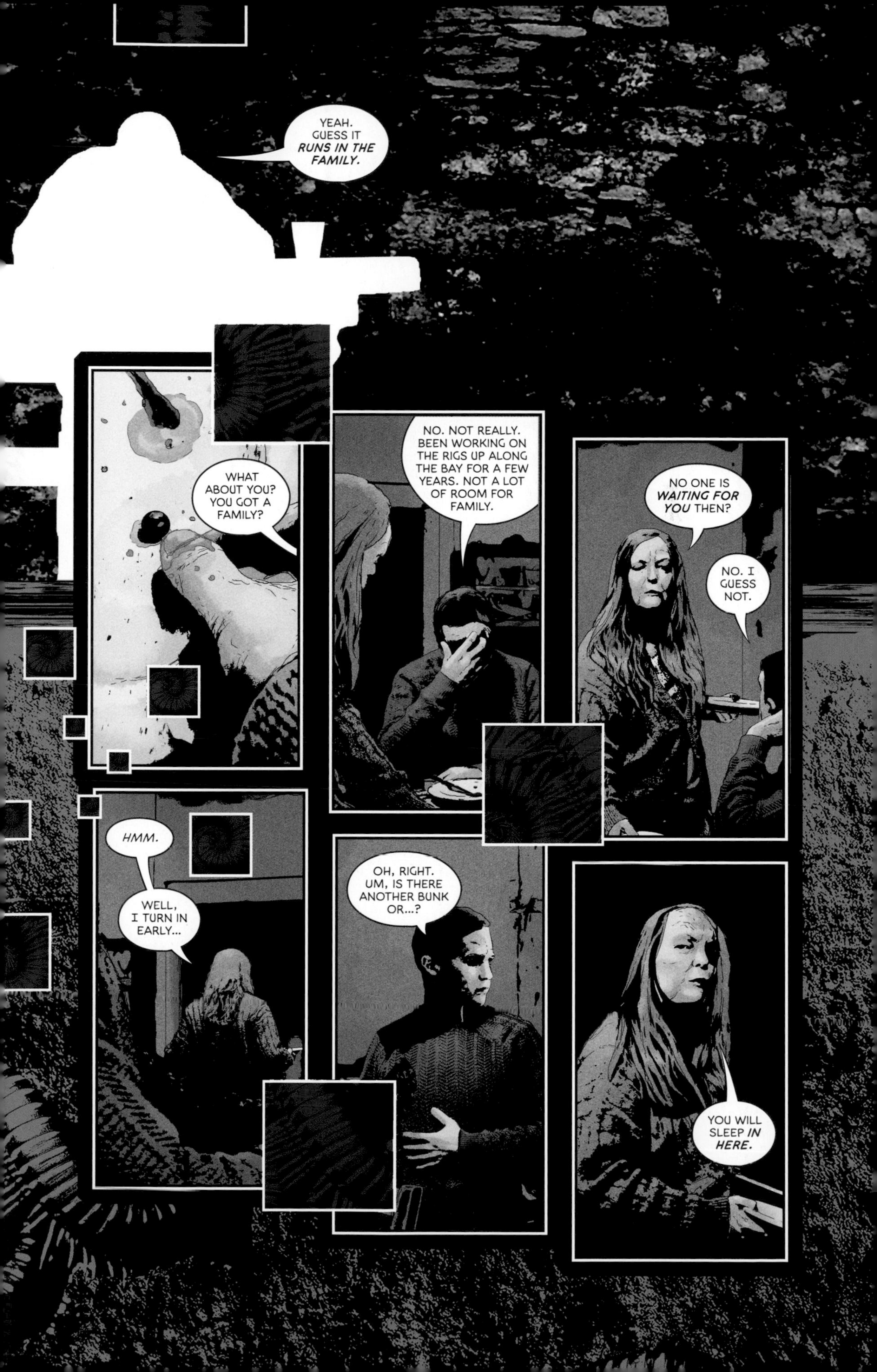
YEAH. GUESS IT RUNS IN THE FAMILY.
WHAT ABOUT YOU? YOU GOT A FAMILY?
NO. NOT REALLY. BEEN WORKING ON THE RIGS UP ALONG THE BAY FOR A FEW YEARS. NOT A LOT OF ROOM FOR FAMILY.
NO ONE IS WAITING FOR YOU THEN?
NO. I GUESS NOT.
HMM.
WELL, I TURN IN EARLY...
OH, RIGHT. UM, IS THERE ANOTHER BUNK OR...?
YOU WILL SLEEP IN HERE.

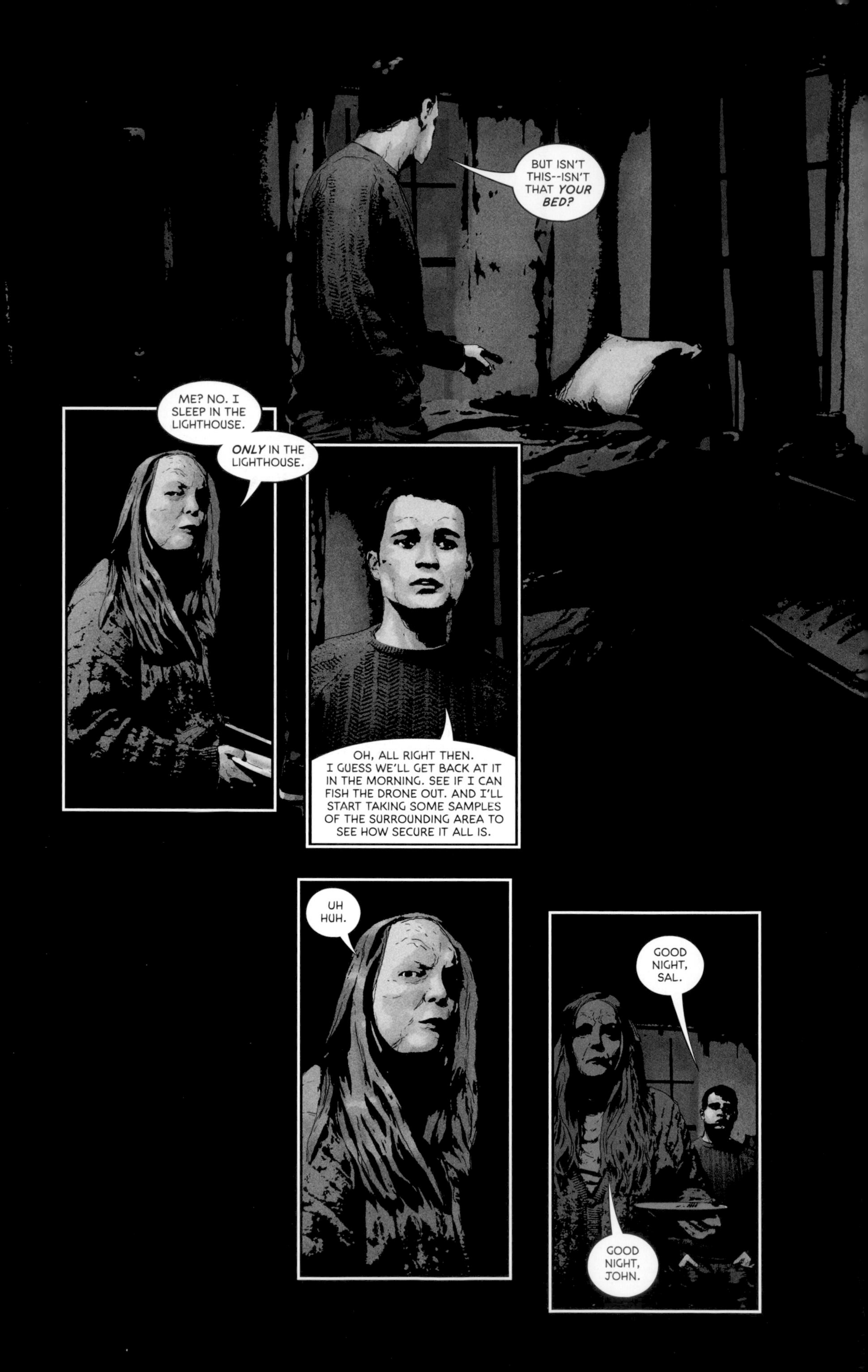
BUT ISN'T THIS--ISN'T THAT *YOUR BED?*
ME? NO. I SLEEP IN THE LIGHTHOUSE.
ONLY IN THE LIGHTHOUSE.
OH, ALL RIGHT THEN. I GUESS WE'LL GET BACK AT IT IN THE MORNING. SEE IF I CAN FISH THE DRONE OUT. AND I'LL START TAKING SOME SAMPLES OF THE SURROUNDING AREA TO SEE HOW SECURE IT ALL IS.
UH HUH.
GOOD NIGHT, SAL.
GOOD NIGHT, JOHN.

no signal
09:43 p.m.
swipe to unlock
no signal
GREAT.

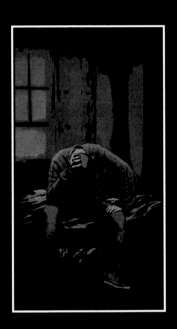

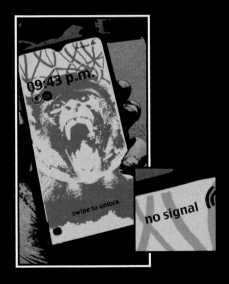

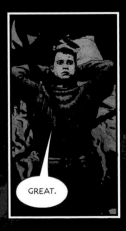

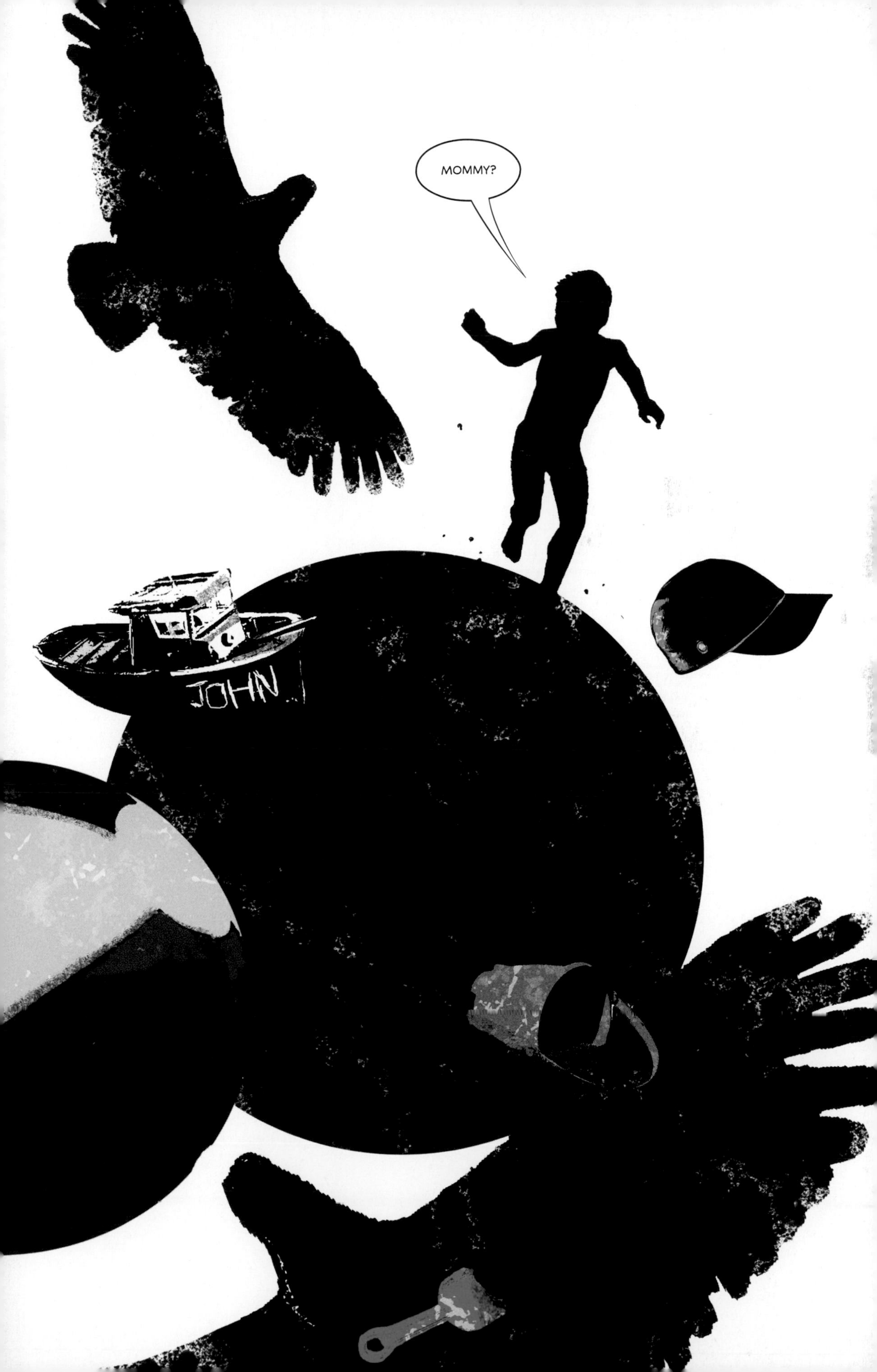
MOMMY?
JOHN

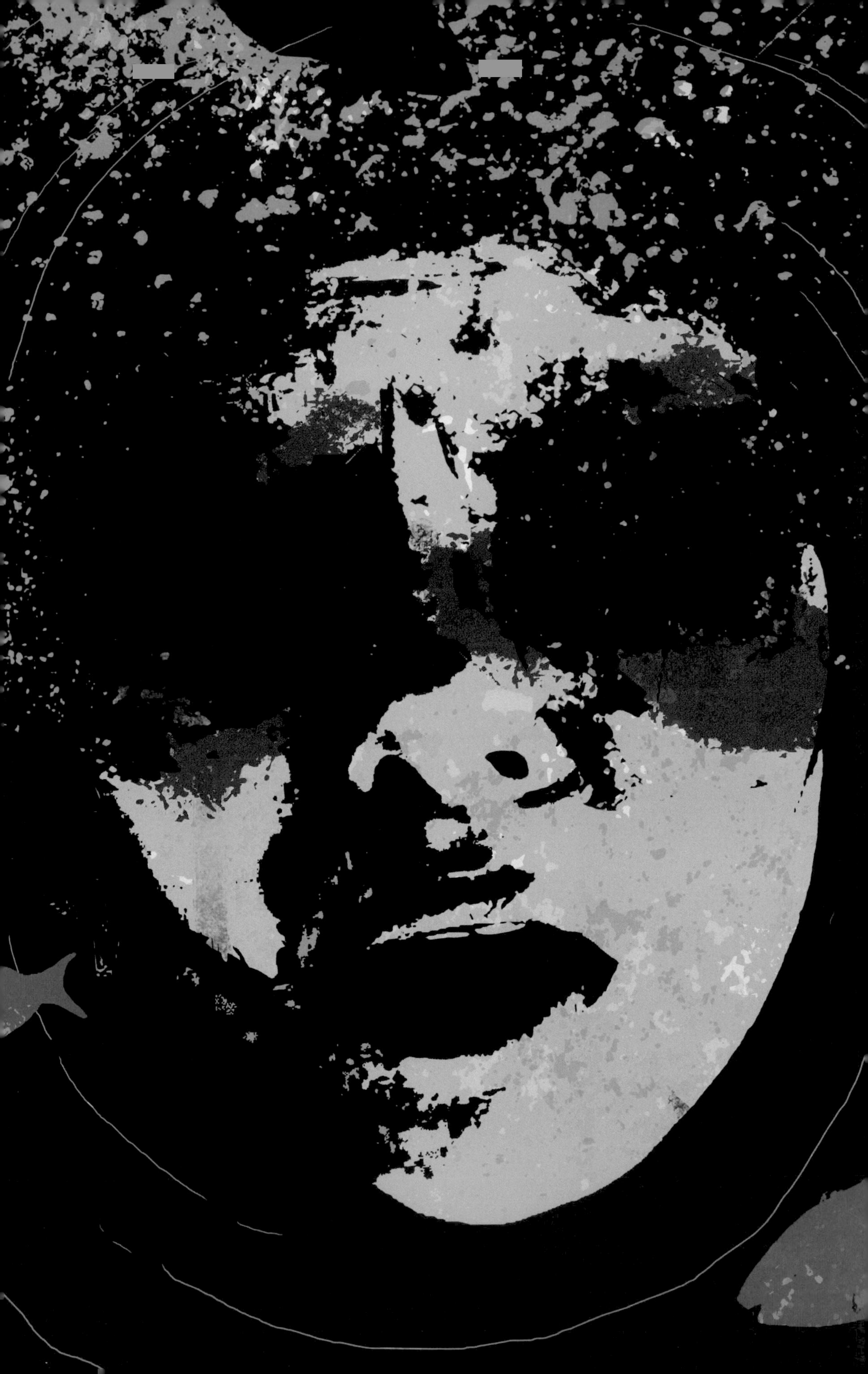

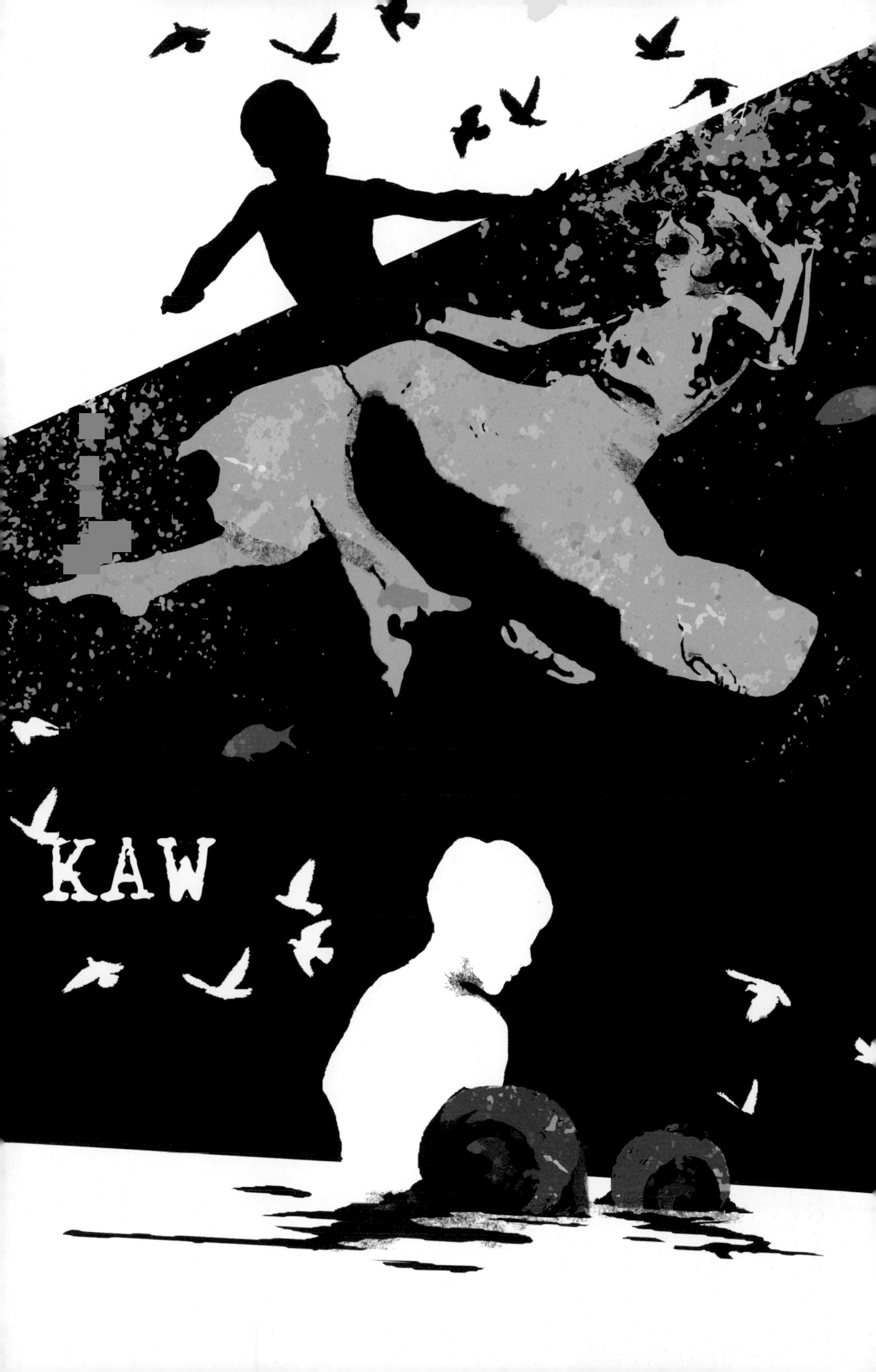
KAW

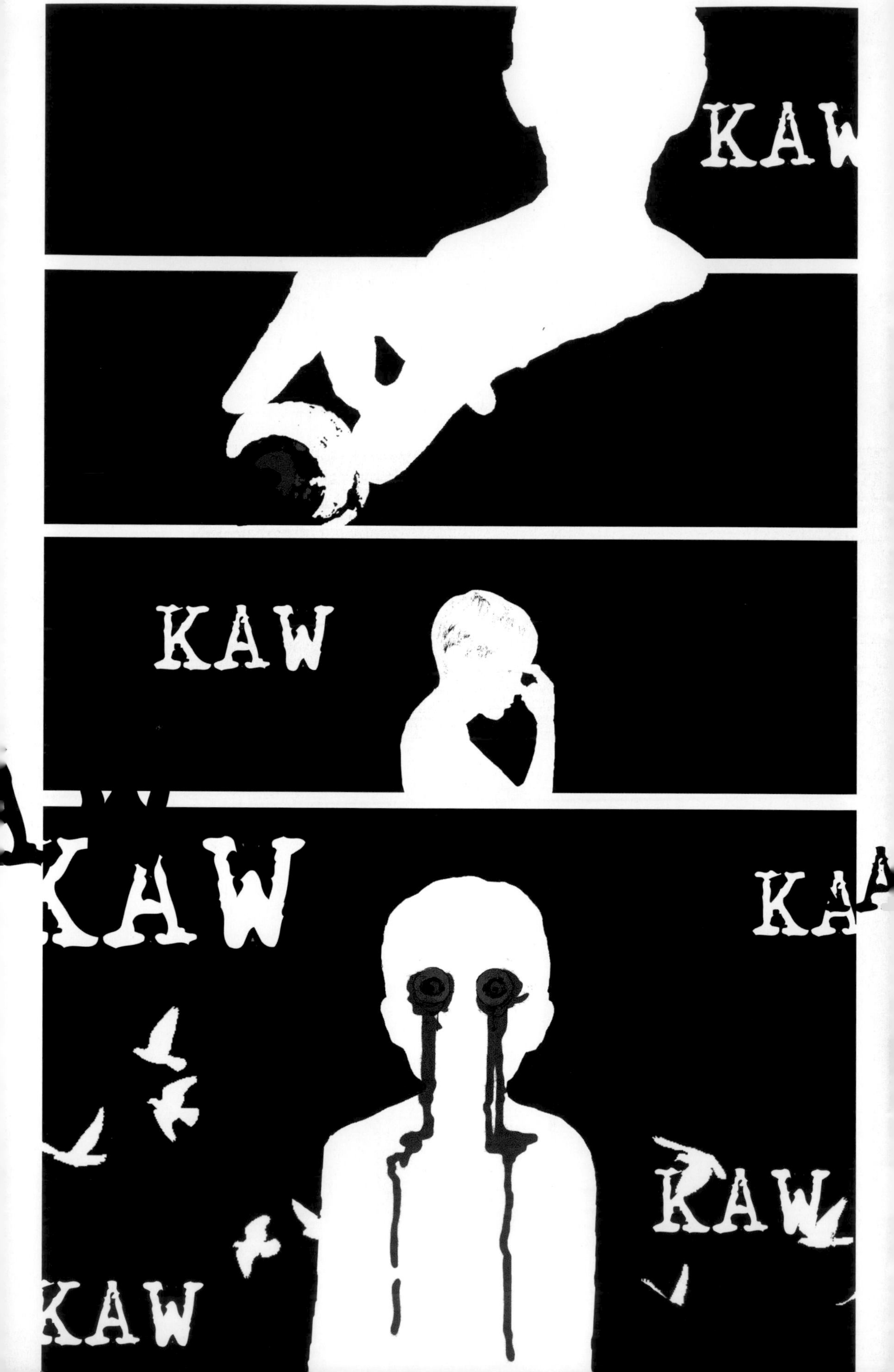
KAW
KAW
KAW
KAW
KAW

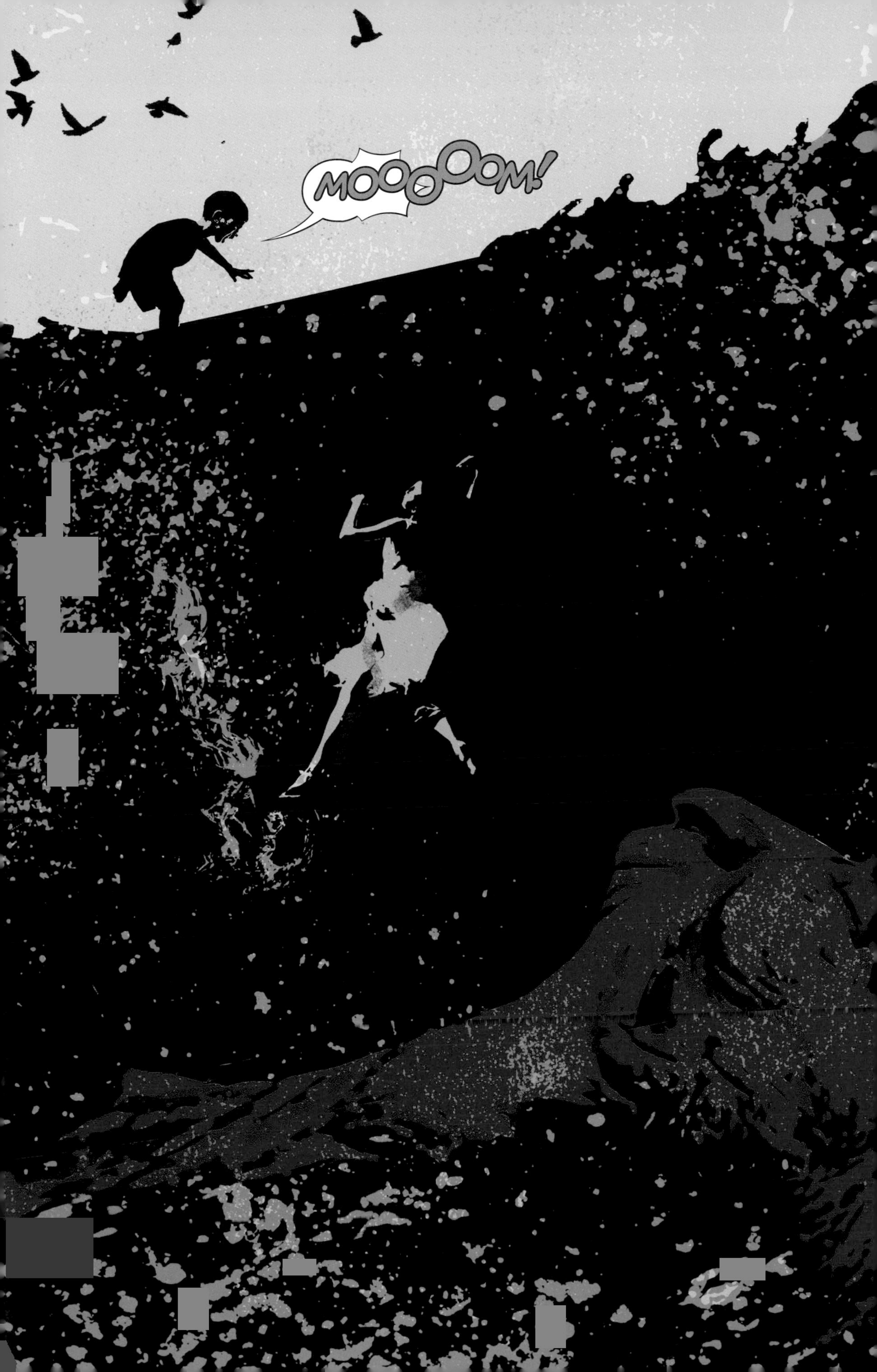
MOOOOOOM!

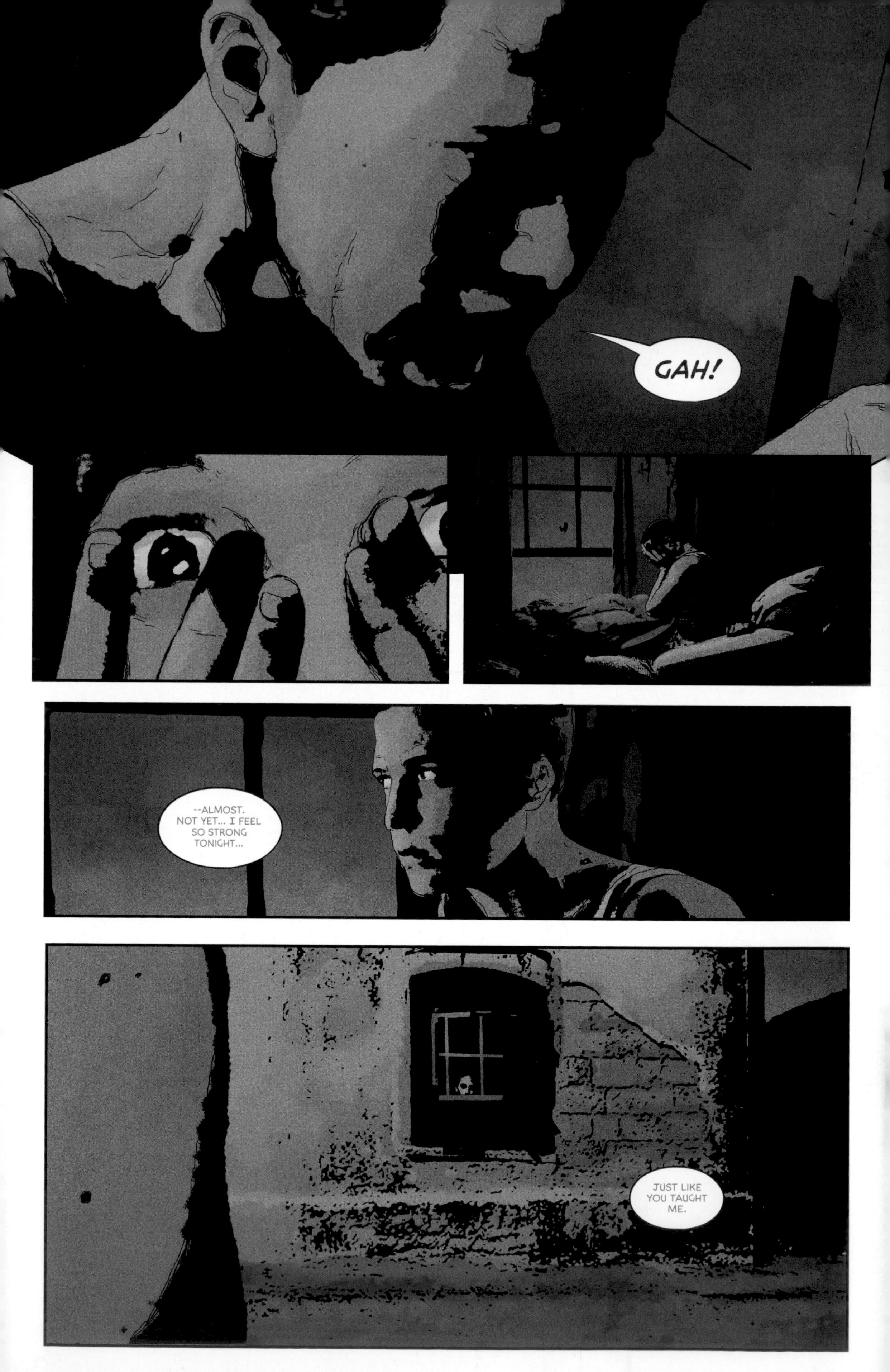
GAH!
--ALMOST. NOT YET... I FEEL SO STRONG TONIGHT...
JUST LIKE YOU TAUGHT ME.

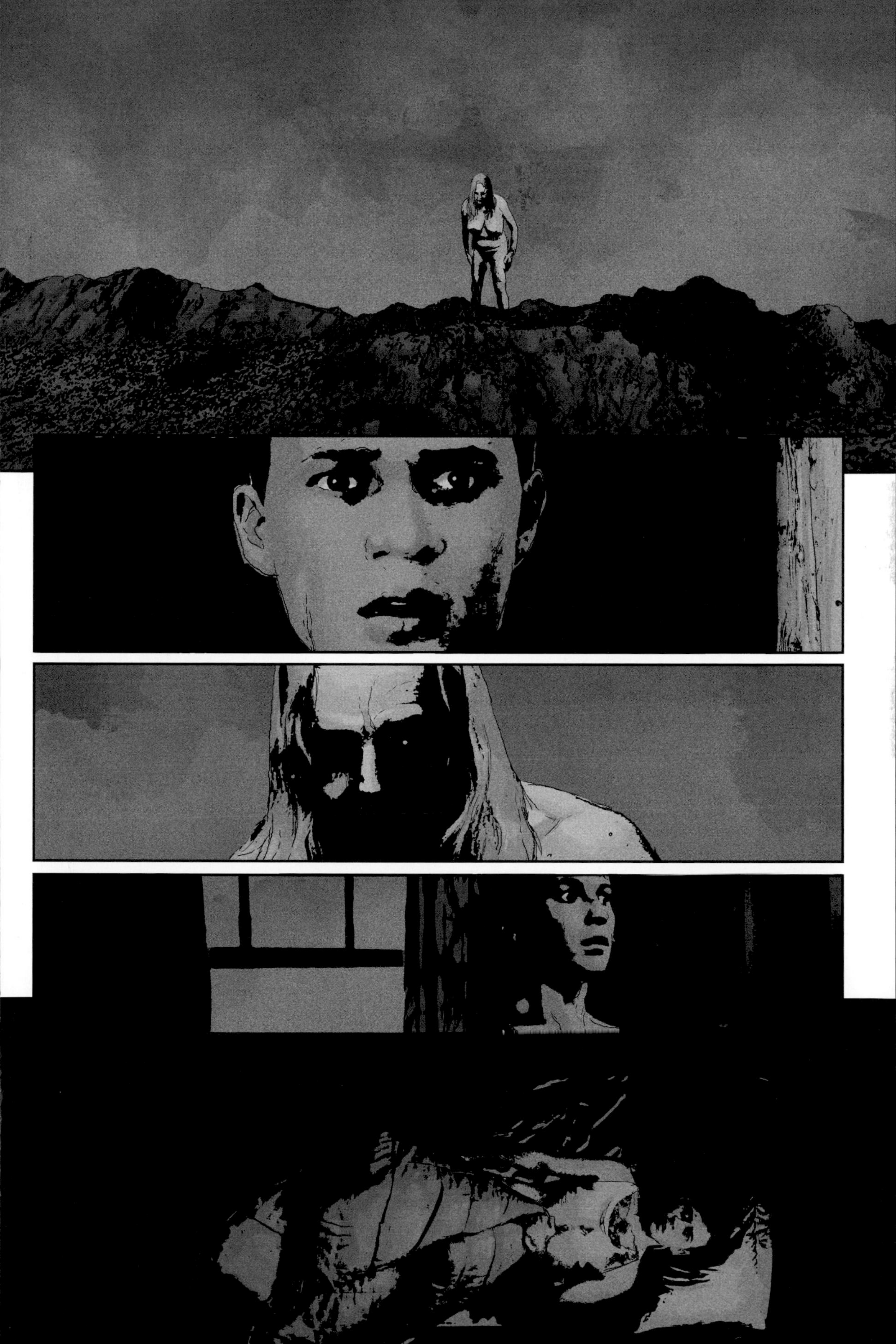

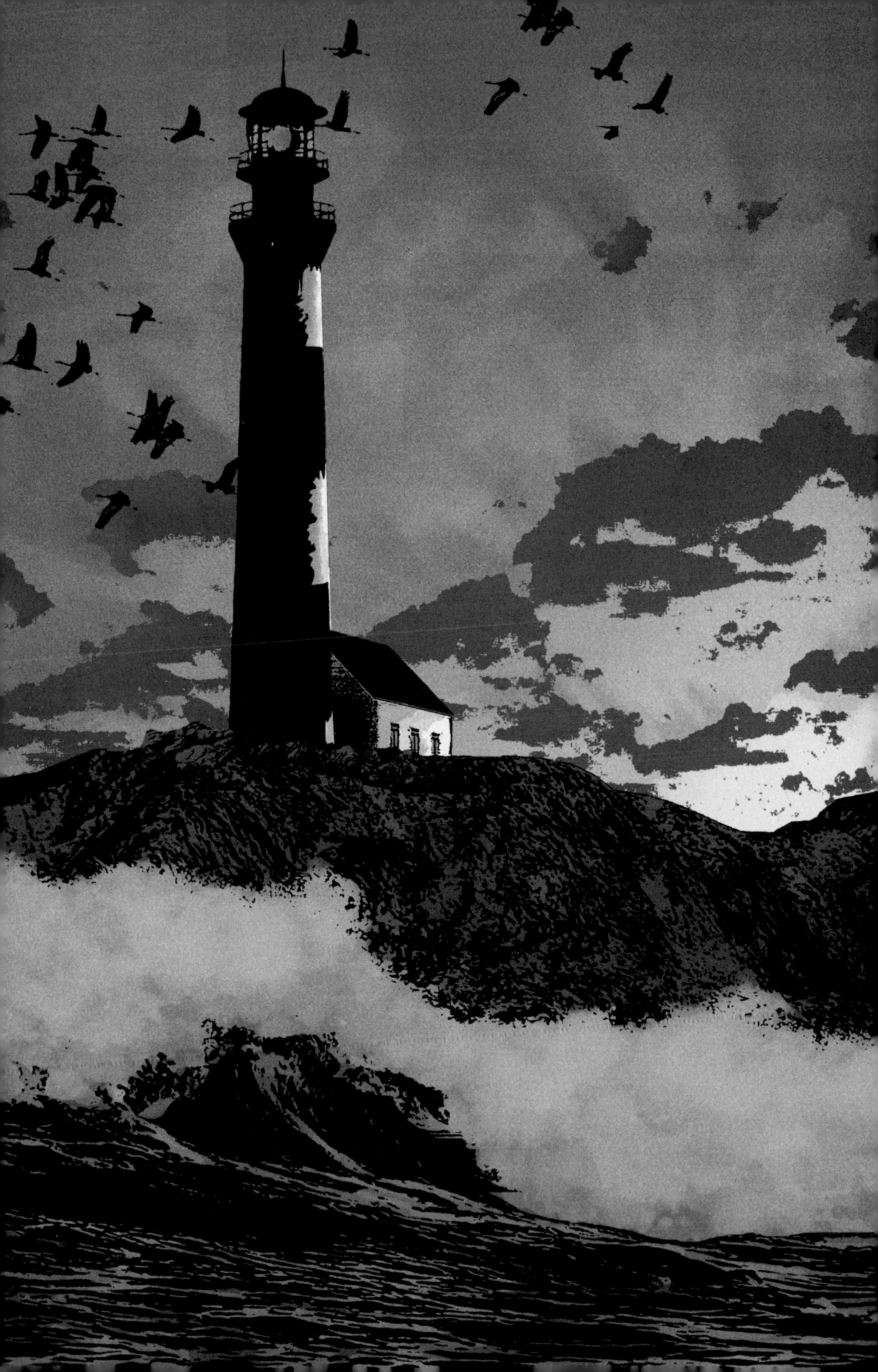

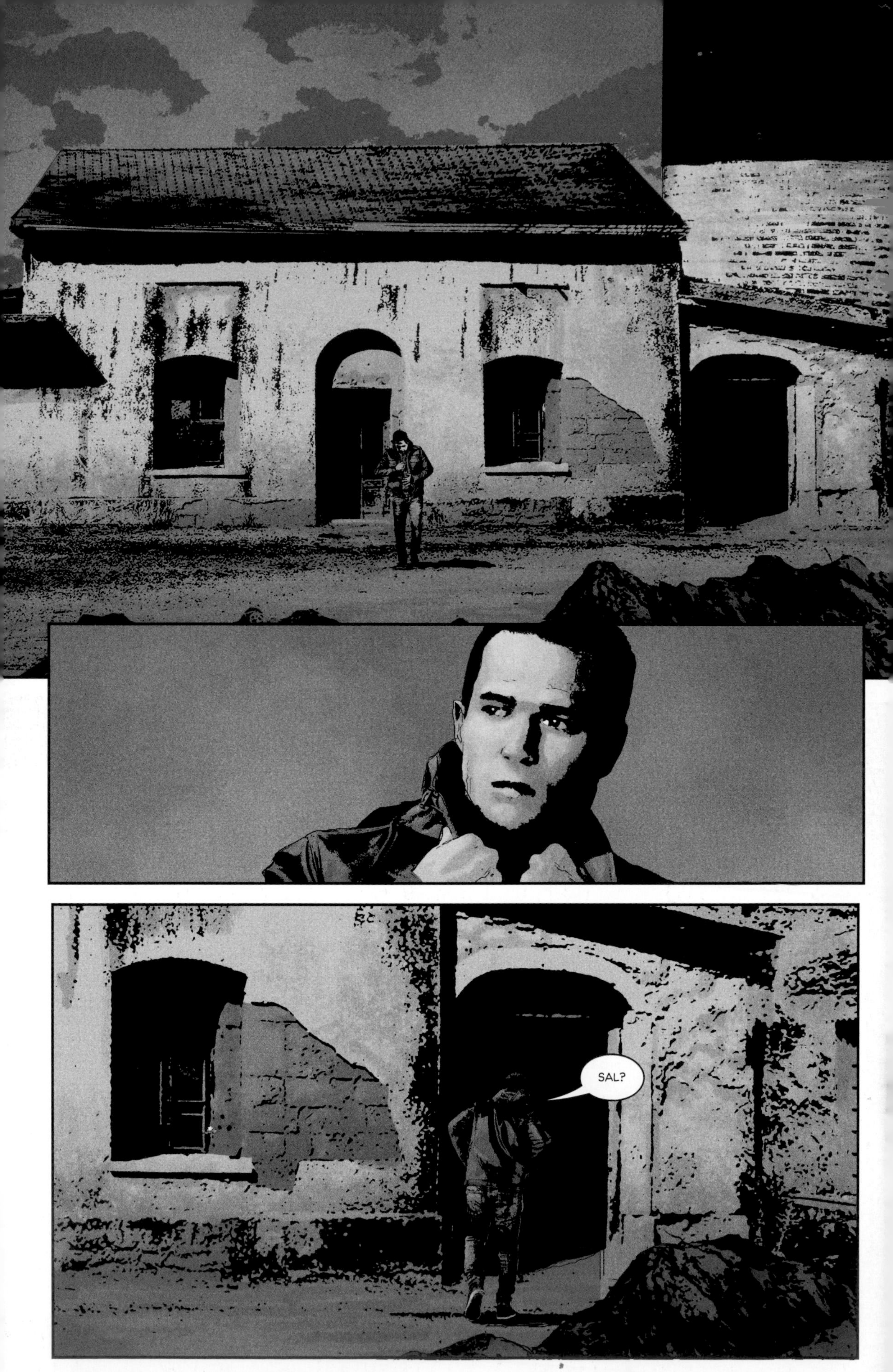
SAL?

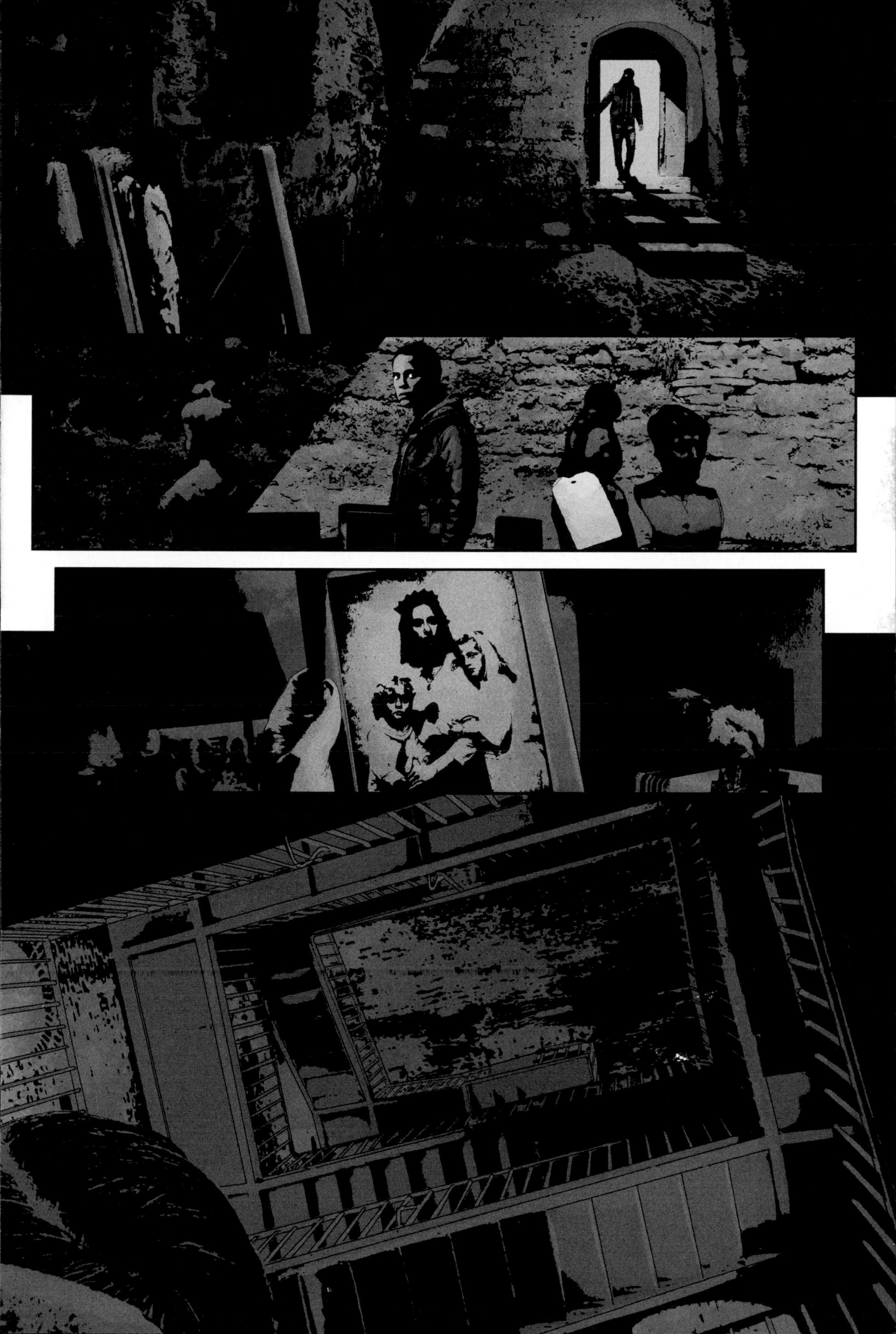

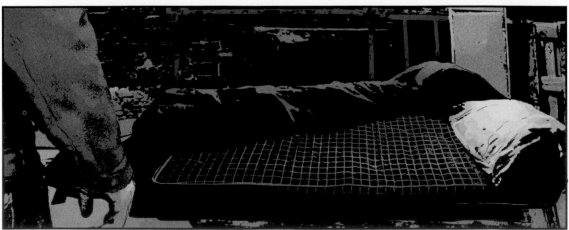

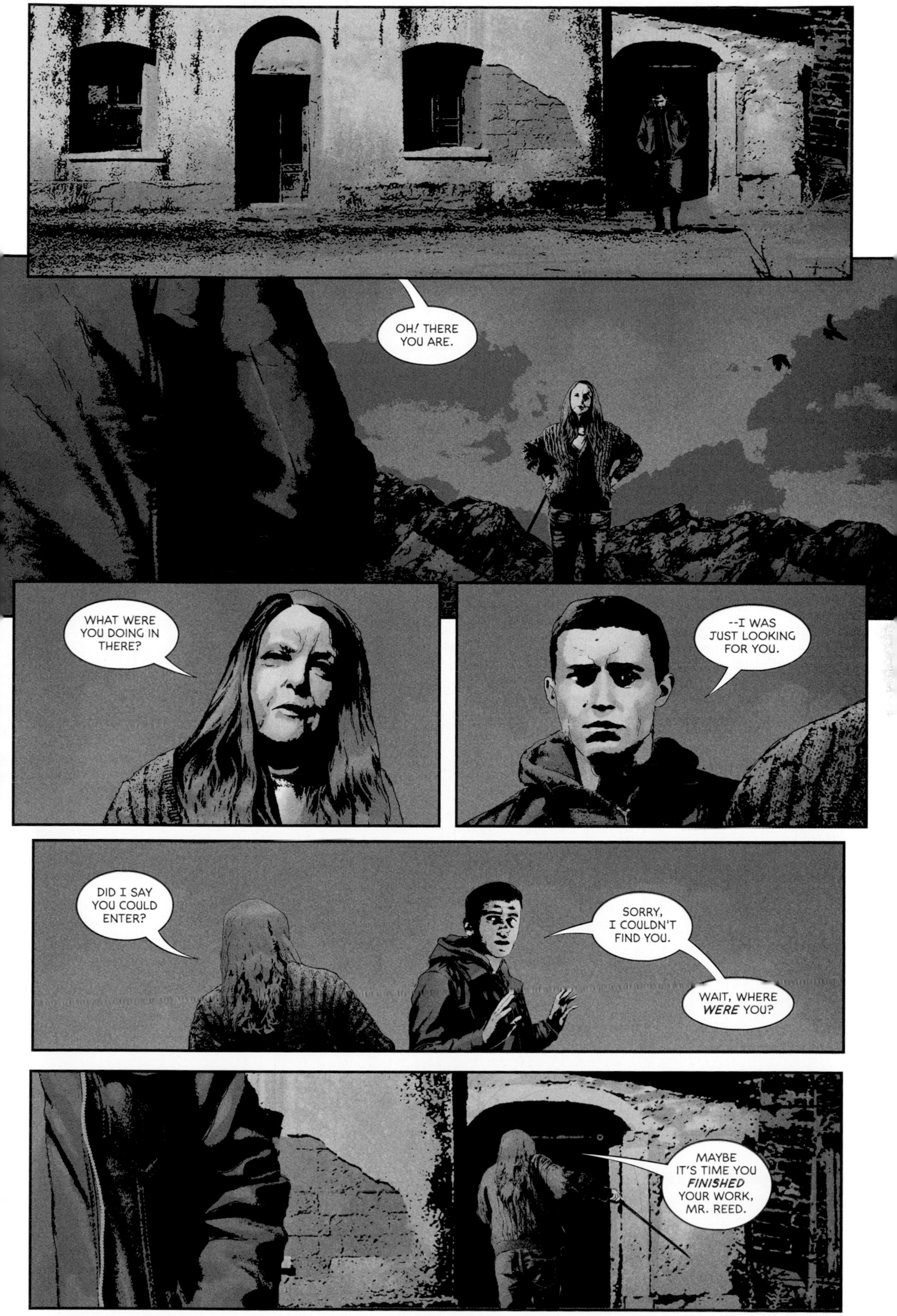
OH! THERE YOU ARE.
WHAT WERE YOU DOING IN THERE?
--I WAS JUST LOOKING FOR YOU.
DID I SAY YOU COULD ENTER?
SORRY, I COULDN'T FIND YOU.
WAIT, WHERE *WERE* YOU?
MAYBE IT'S TIME YOU ***FINISHED*** YOUR WORK, MR. REED.

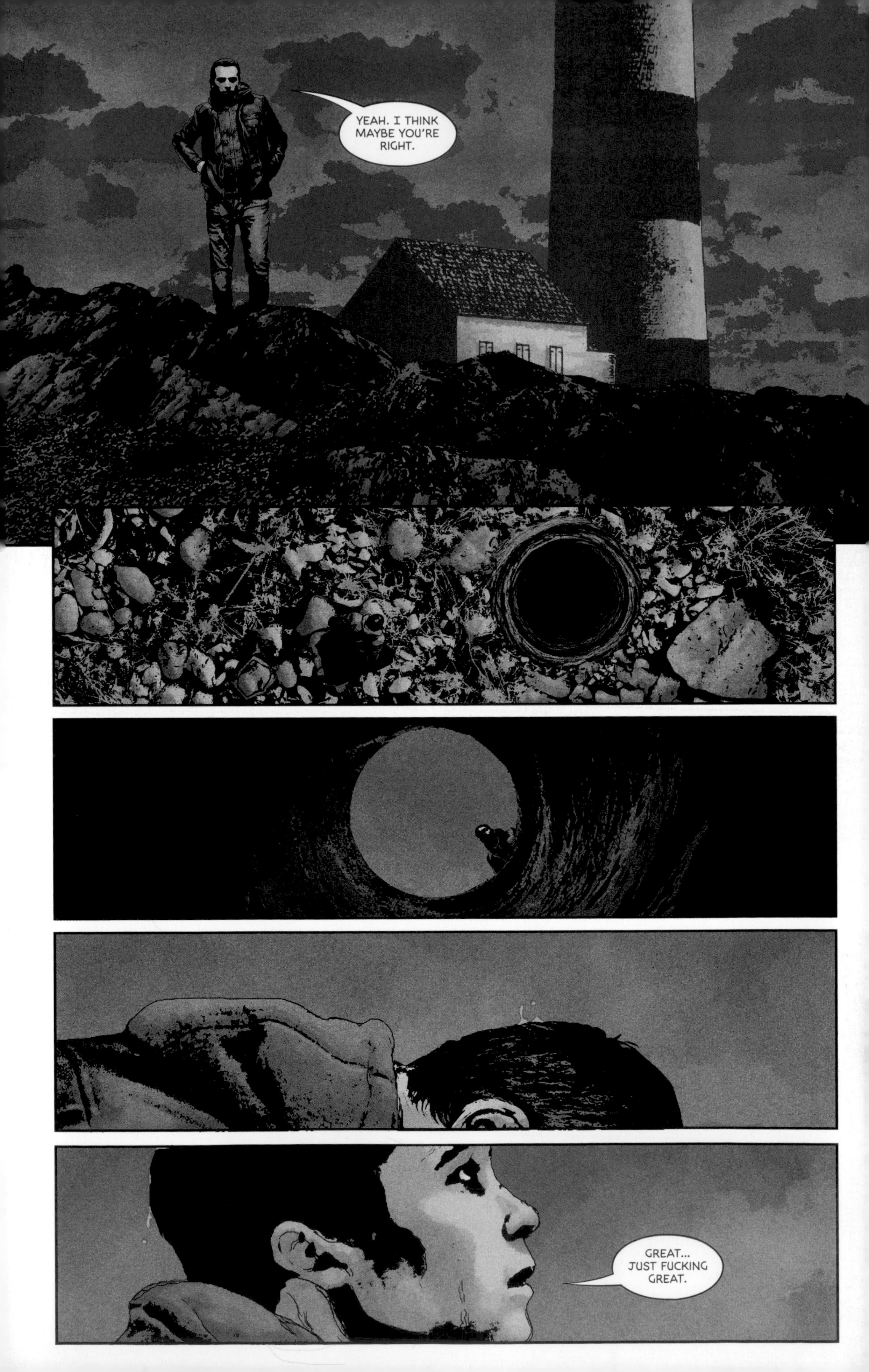
YEAH. I THINK MAYBE YOU'RE RIGHT.
GREAT... JUST FUCKING GREAT.

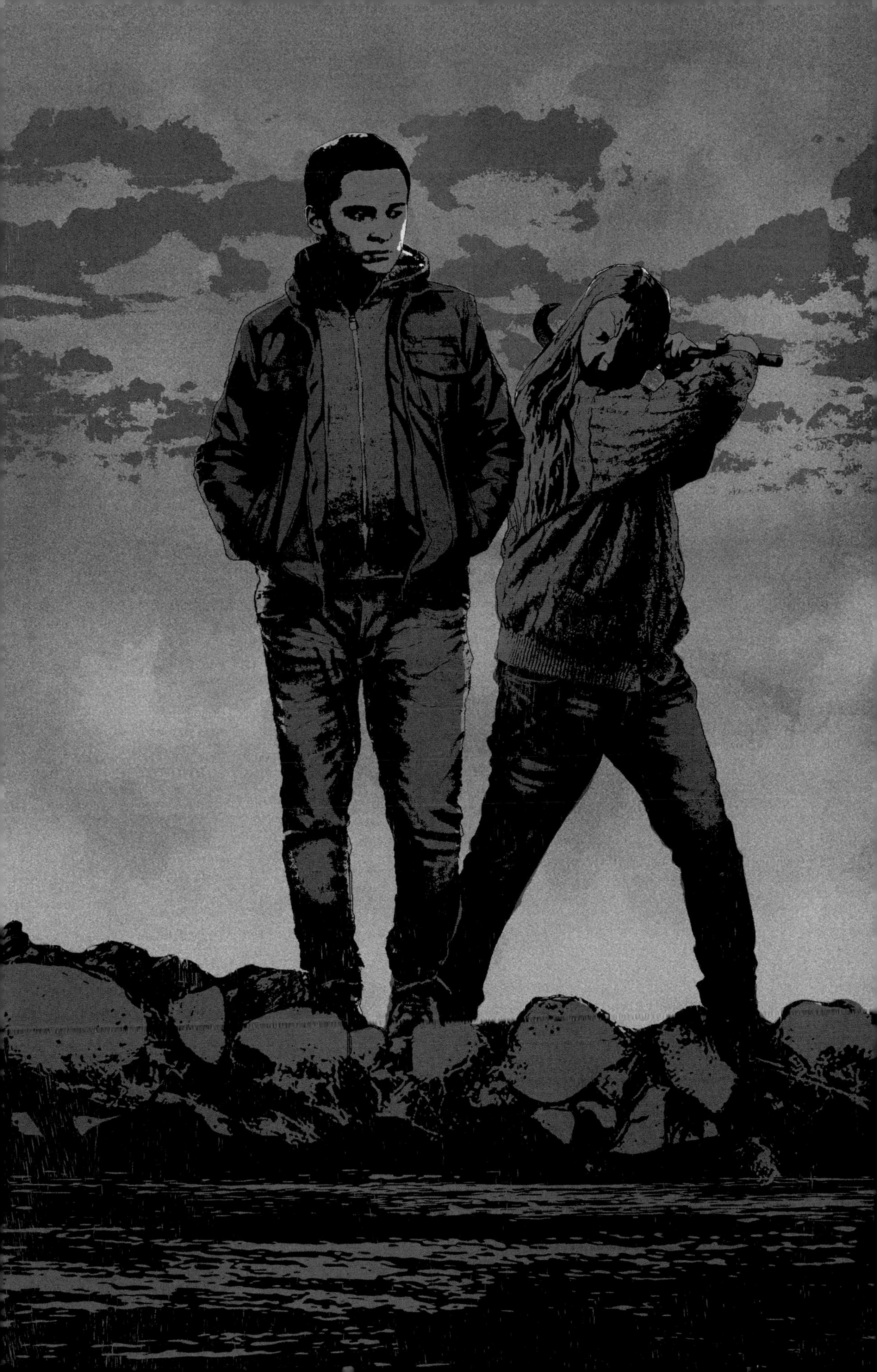

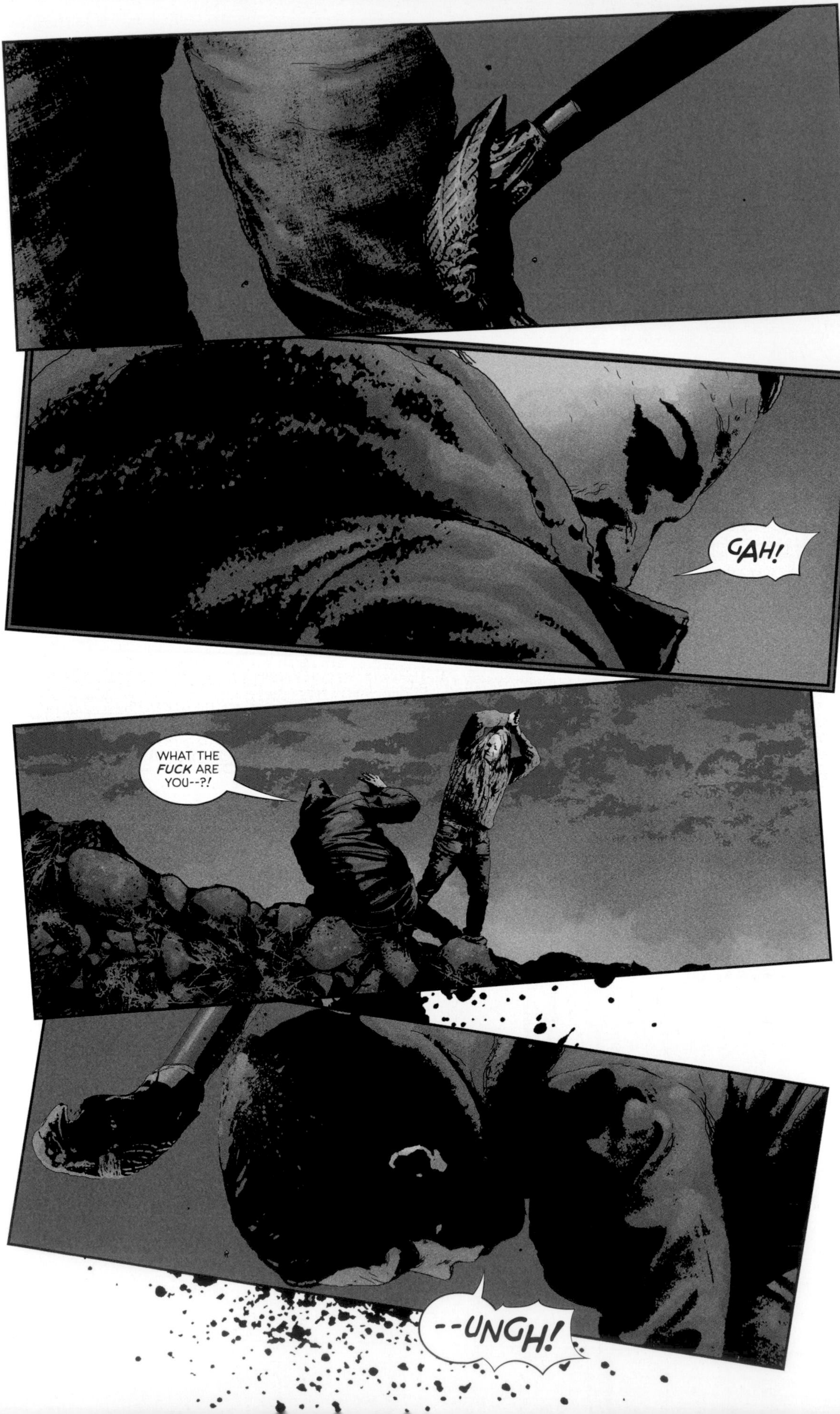
GAH!
WHAT THE *FUCK* ARE YOU--?!
--UNGH!

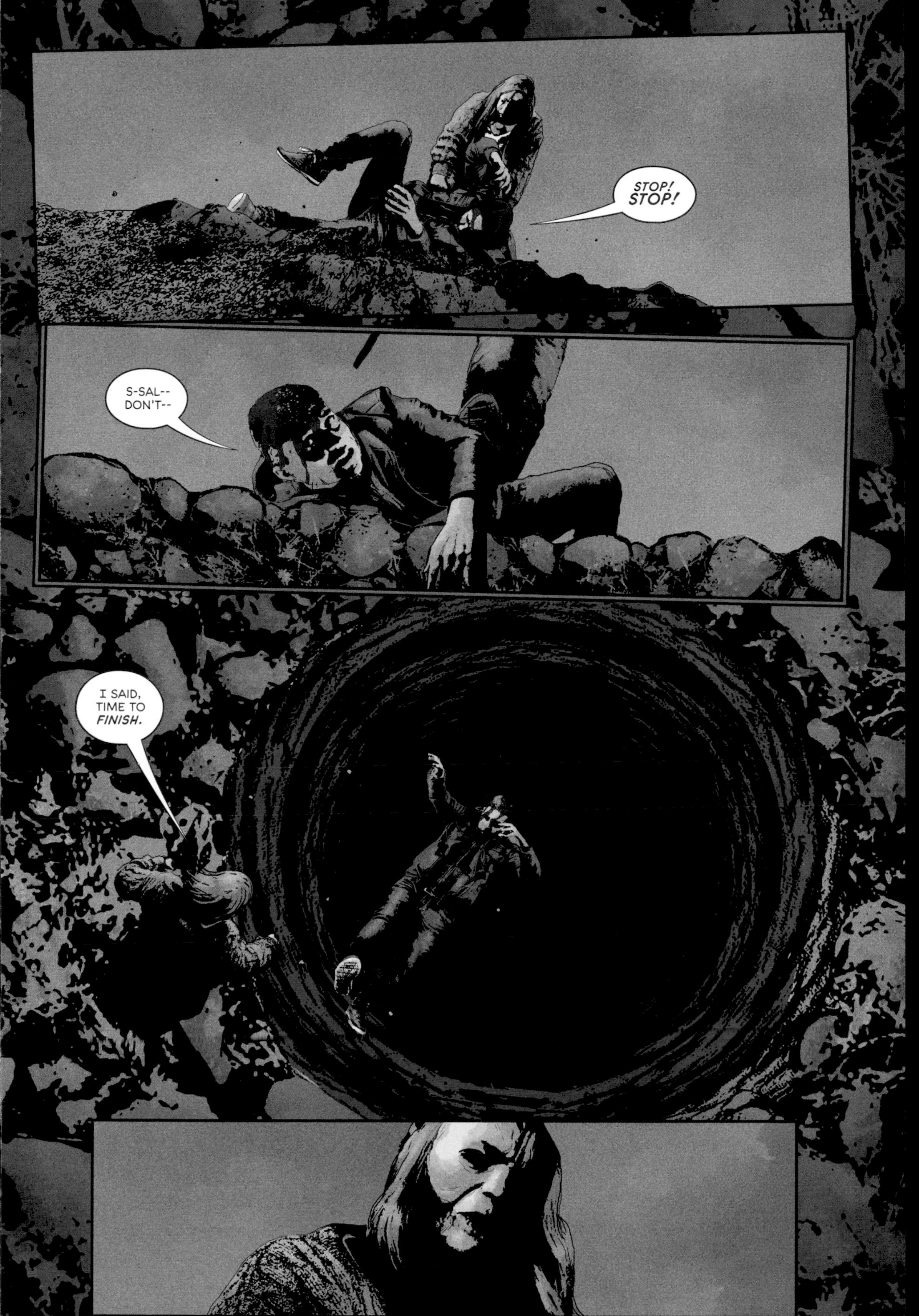
STOP! STOP!
S-SAL-- DON'T--
I SAID, TIME TO FINISH.

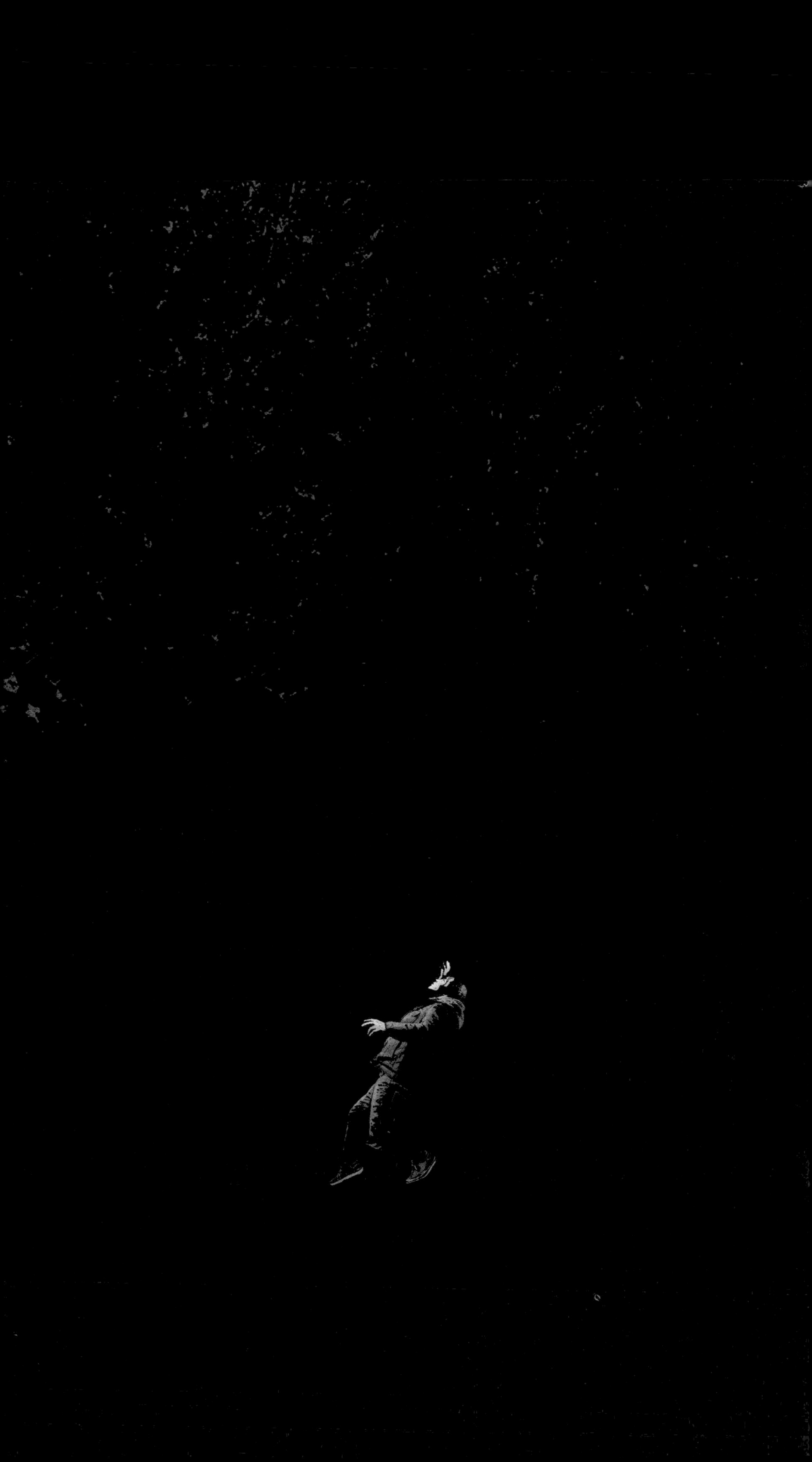

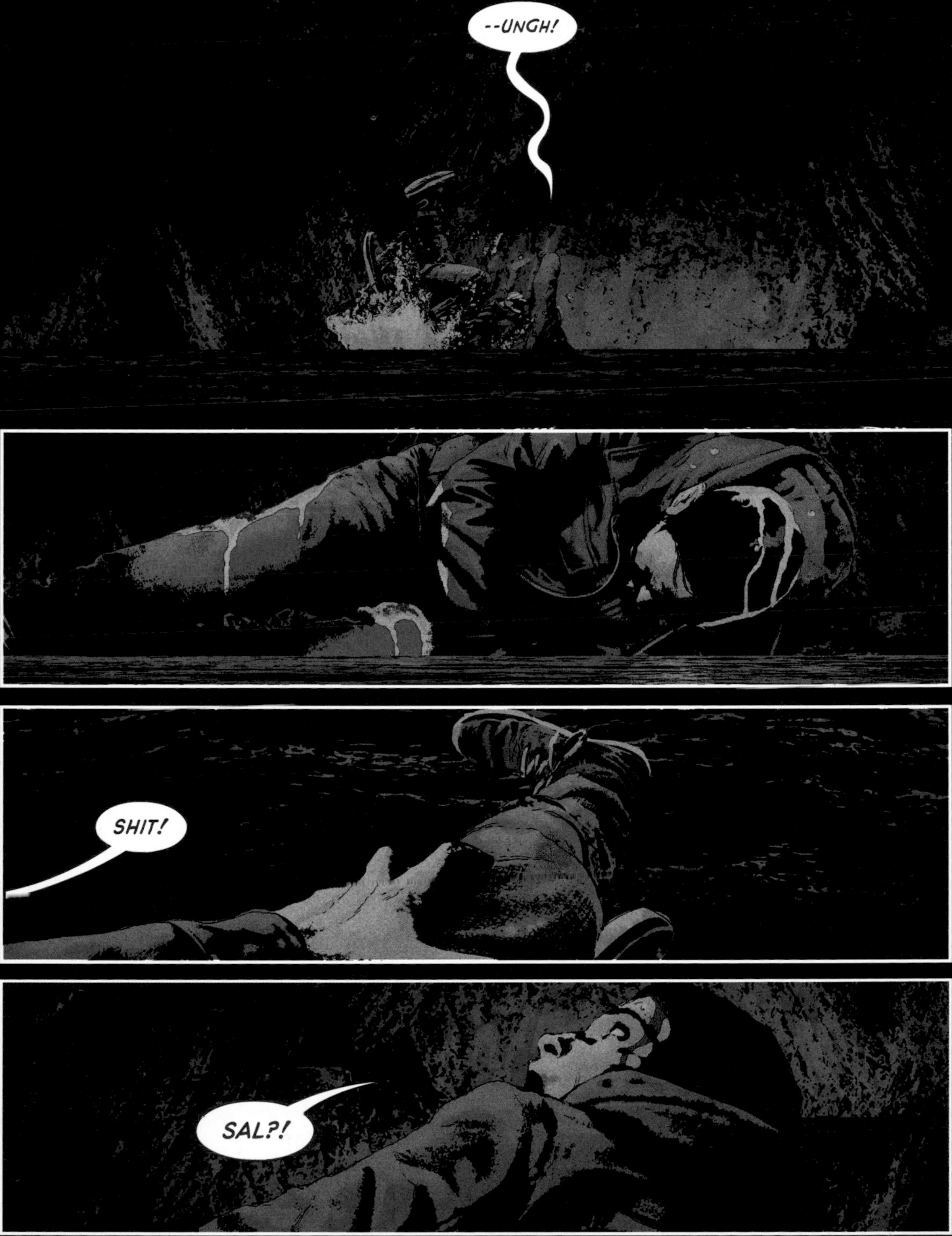
--UNGH!
SHIT!
SAL?!

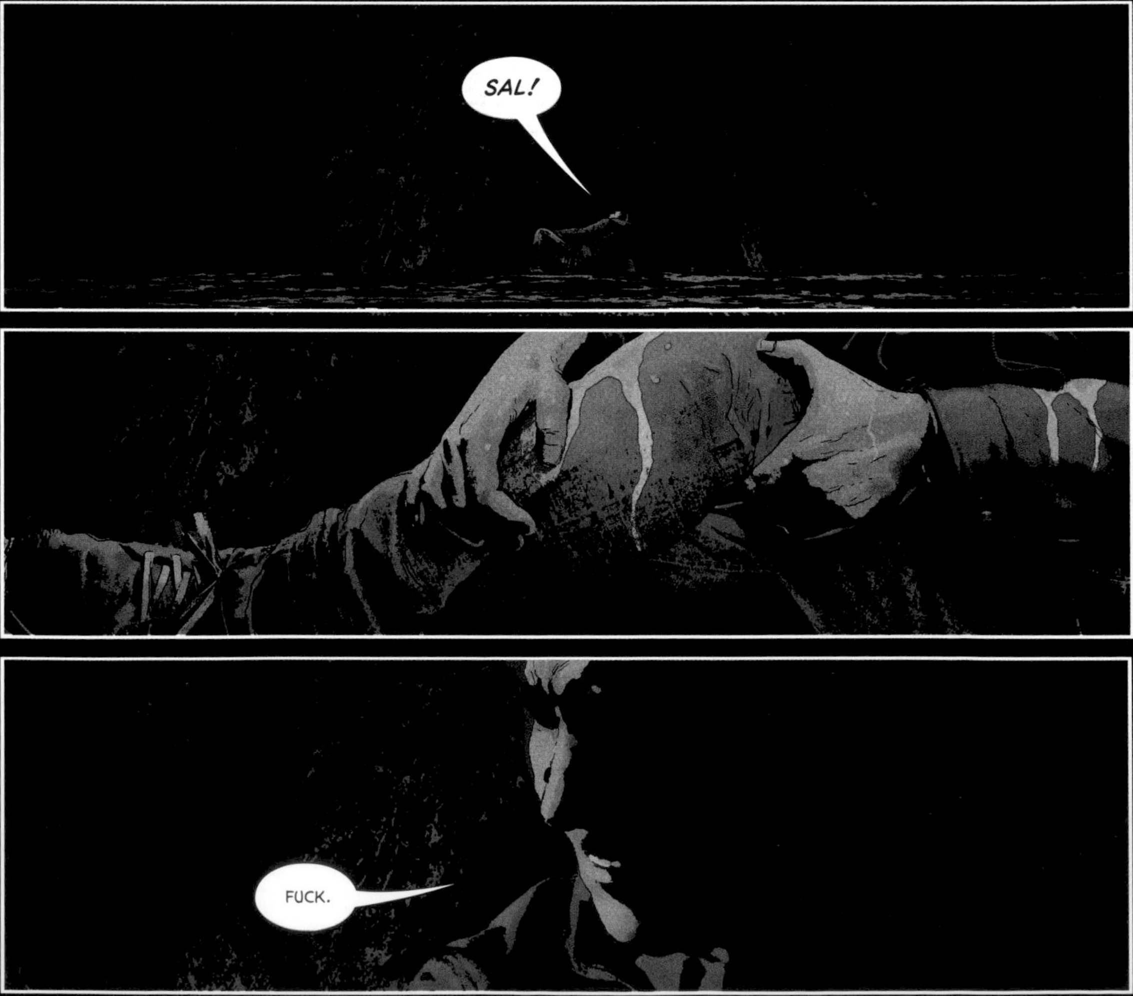
SAL!
FUCK.

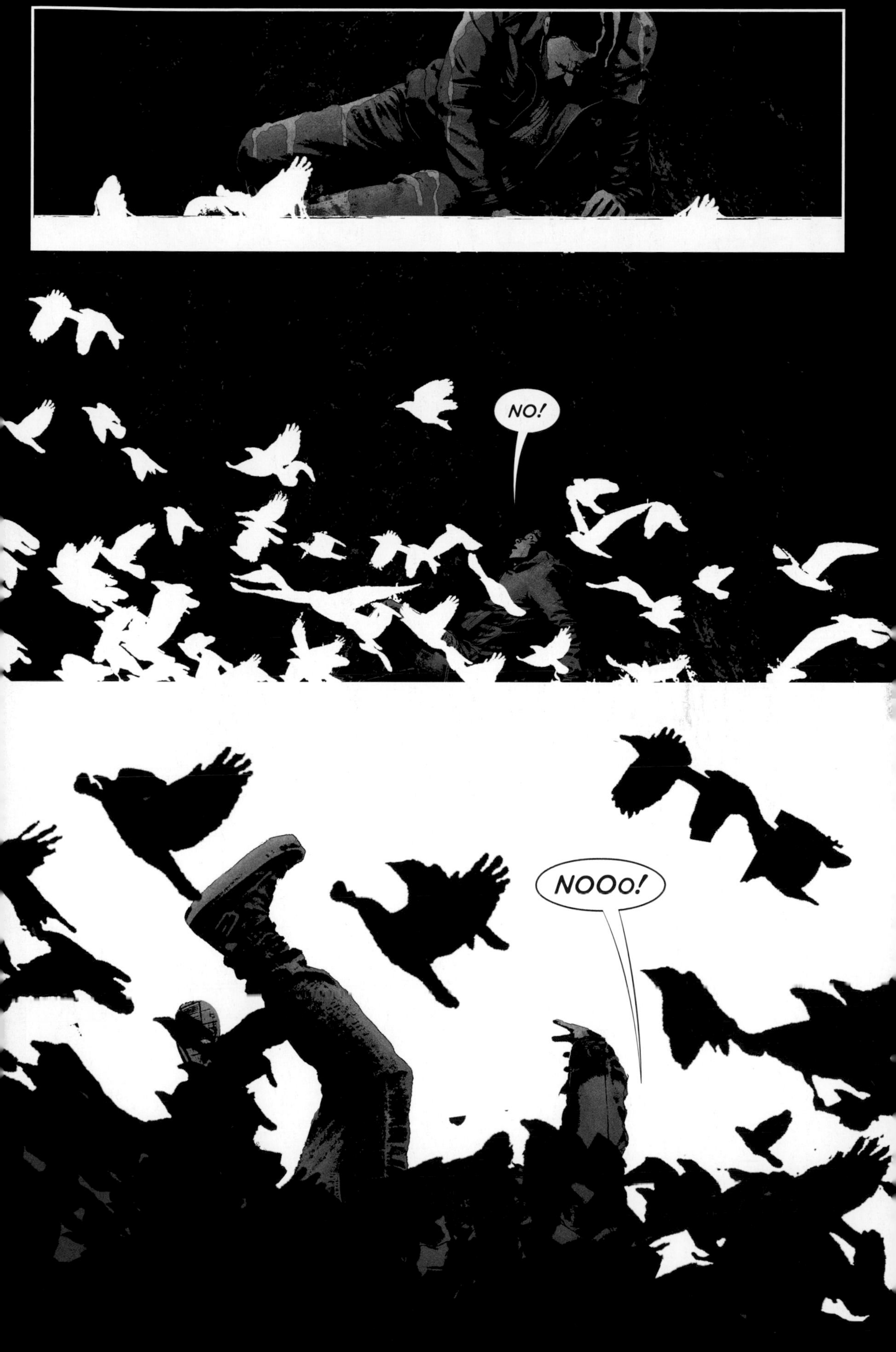
NO!
NOOo!

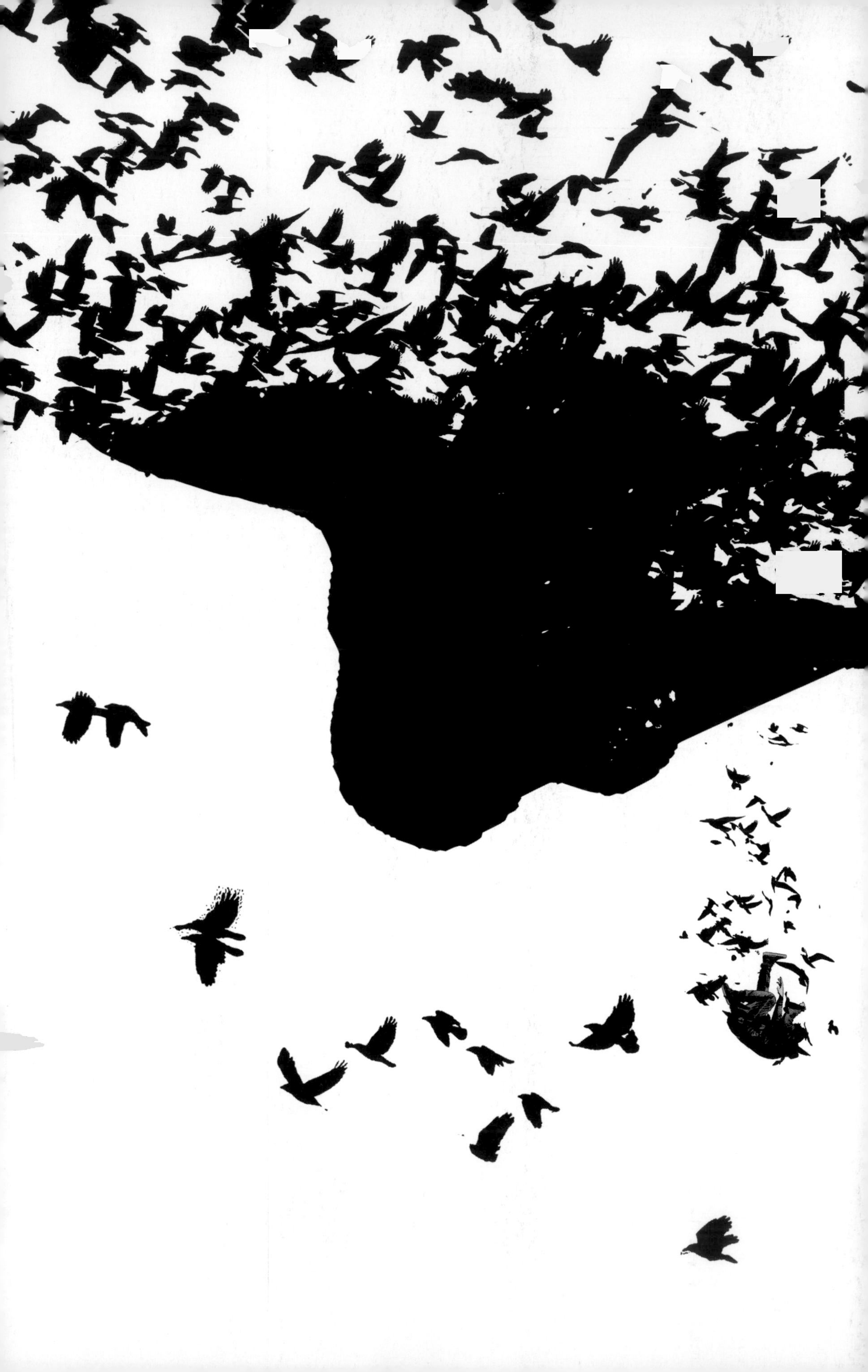

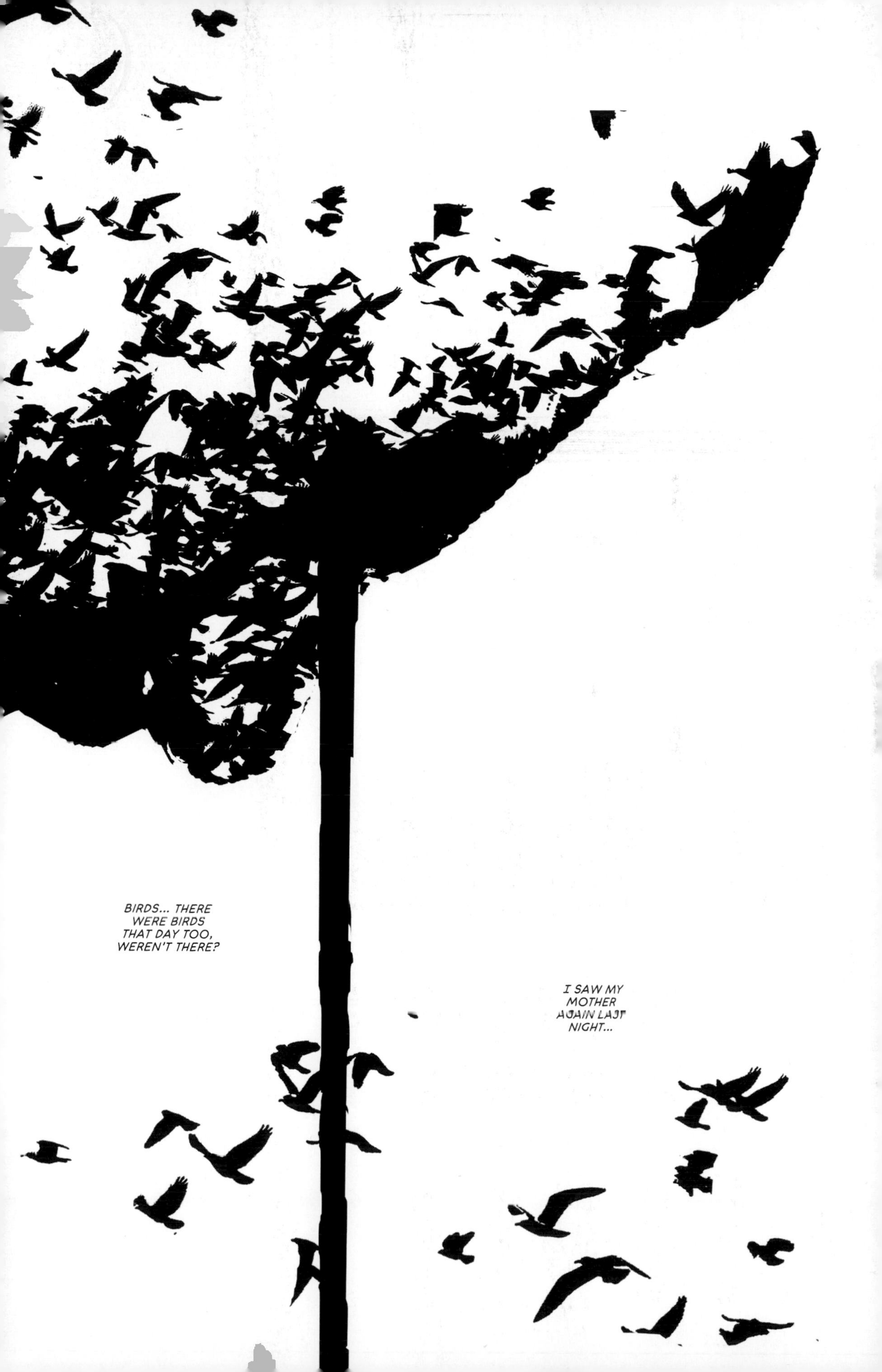
BIRDS... THERE WERE BIRDS THAT DAY TOO, WEREN'T THERE?
I SAW MY MOTHER AGAIN LAST NIGHT...

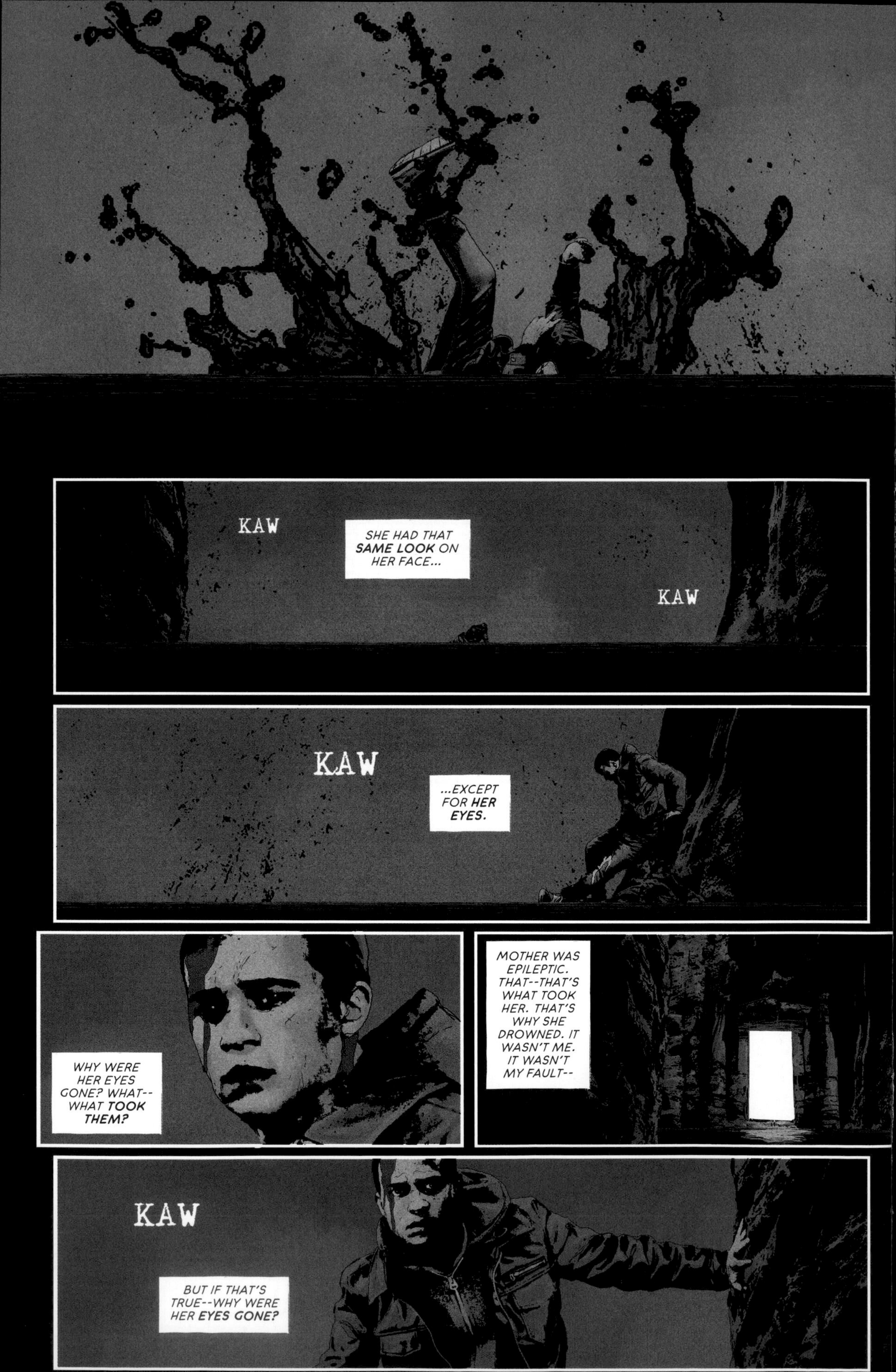
KAW
SHE HAD THAT SAME LOOK ON HER FACE...
KAW
KAW
...EXCEPT FOR HER EYES.
WHY WERE HER EYES GONE? WHAT-- WHAT TOOK THEM?
MOTHER WAS EPILEPTIC. THAT--THAT'S WHAT TOOK HER. THAT'S WHY SHE DROWNED. IT WASN'T ME. IT WASN'T MY FAULT--
KAW
BUT IF THAT'S TRUE--WHY WERE HER EYES GONE?

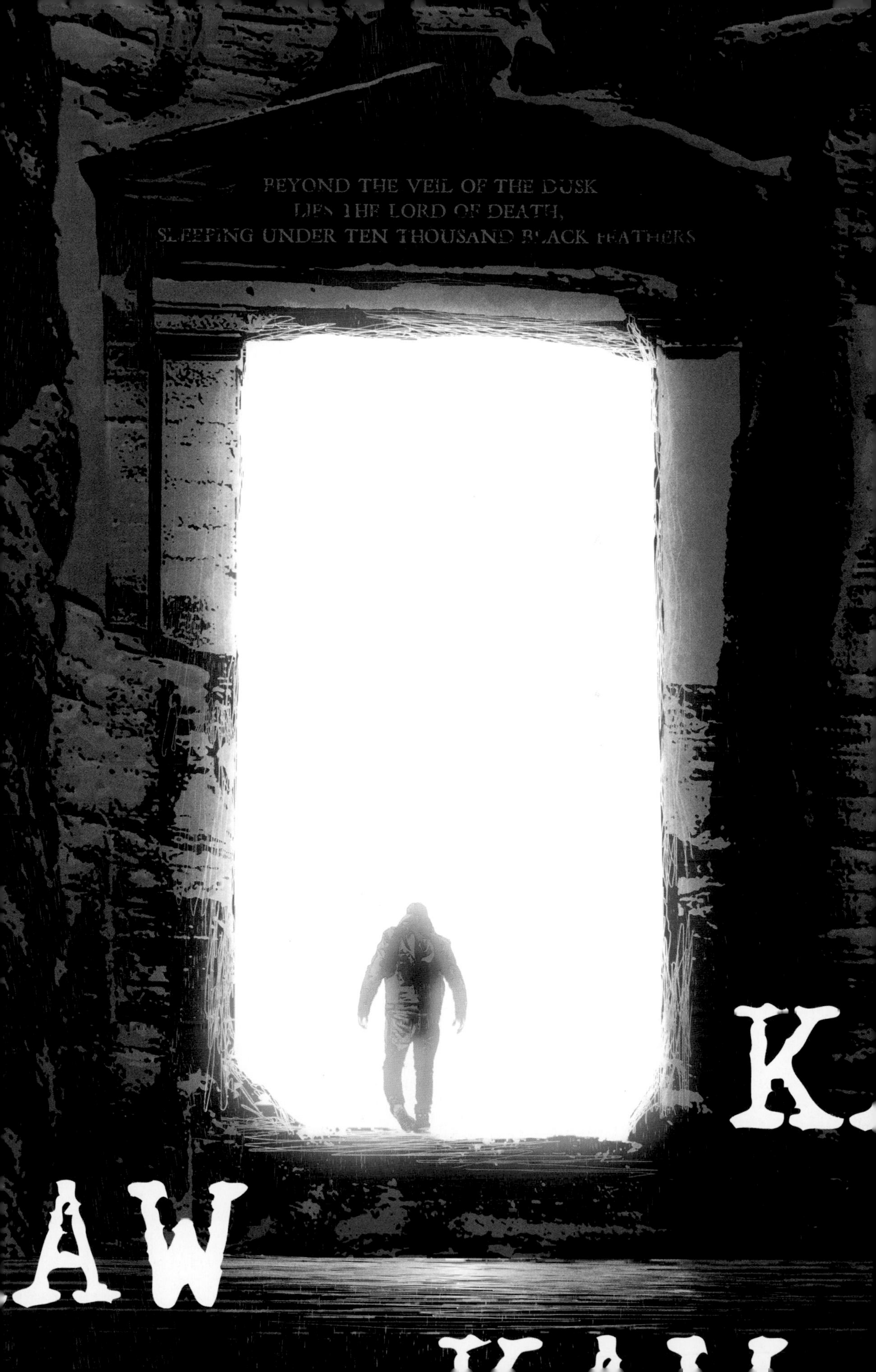
BEYOND THE VEIL OF THE DUSK
LIES THE LORD OF DEATH,
SLEEPING UNDER TEN THOUSAND BLACK FEATHERS

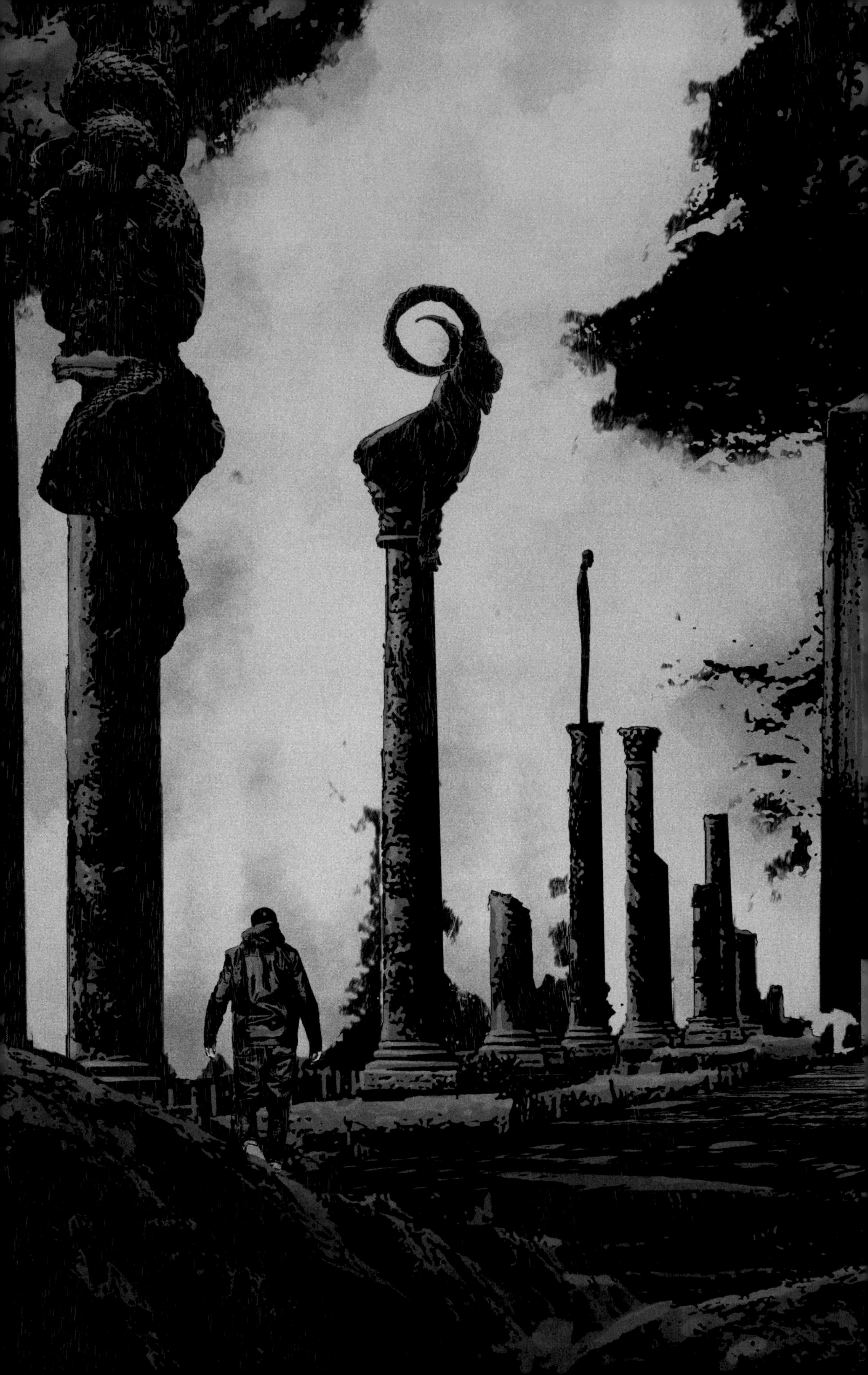

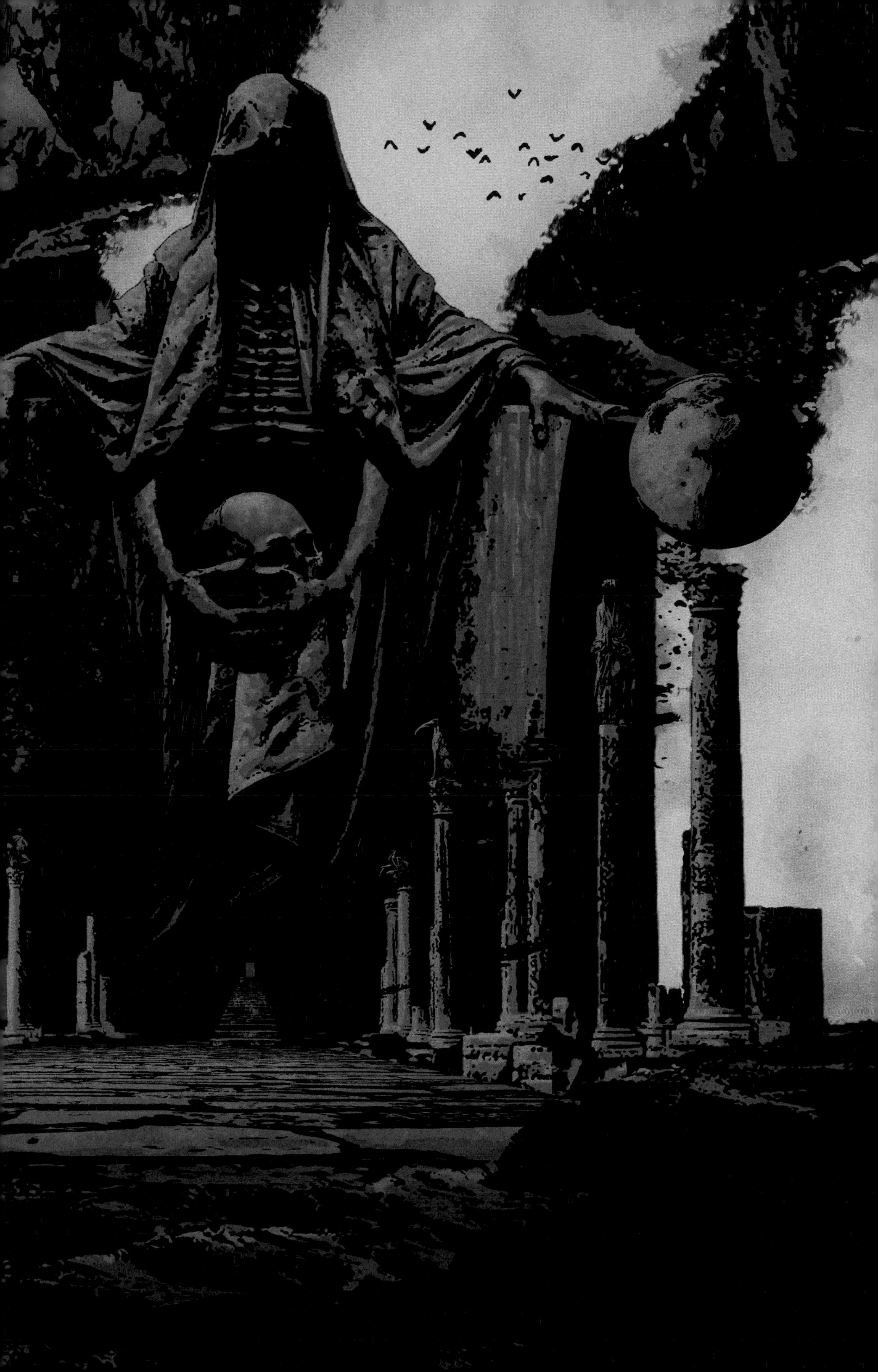

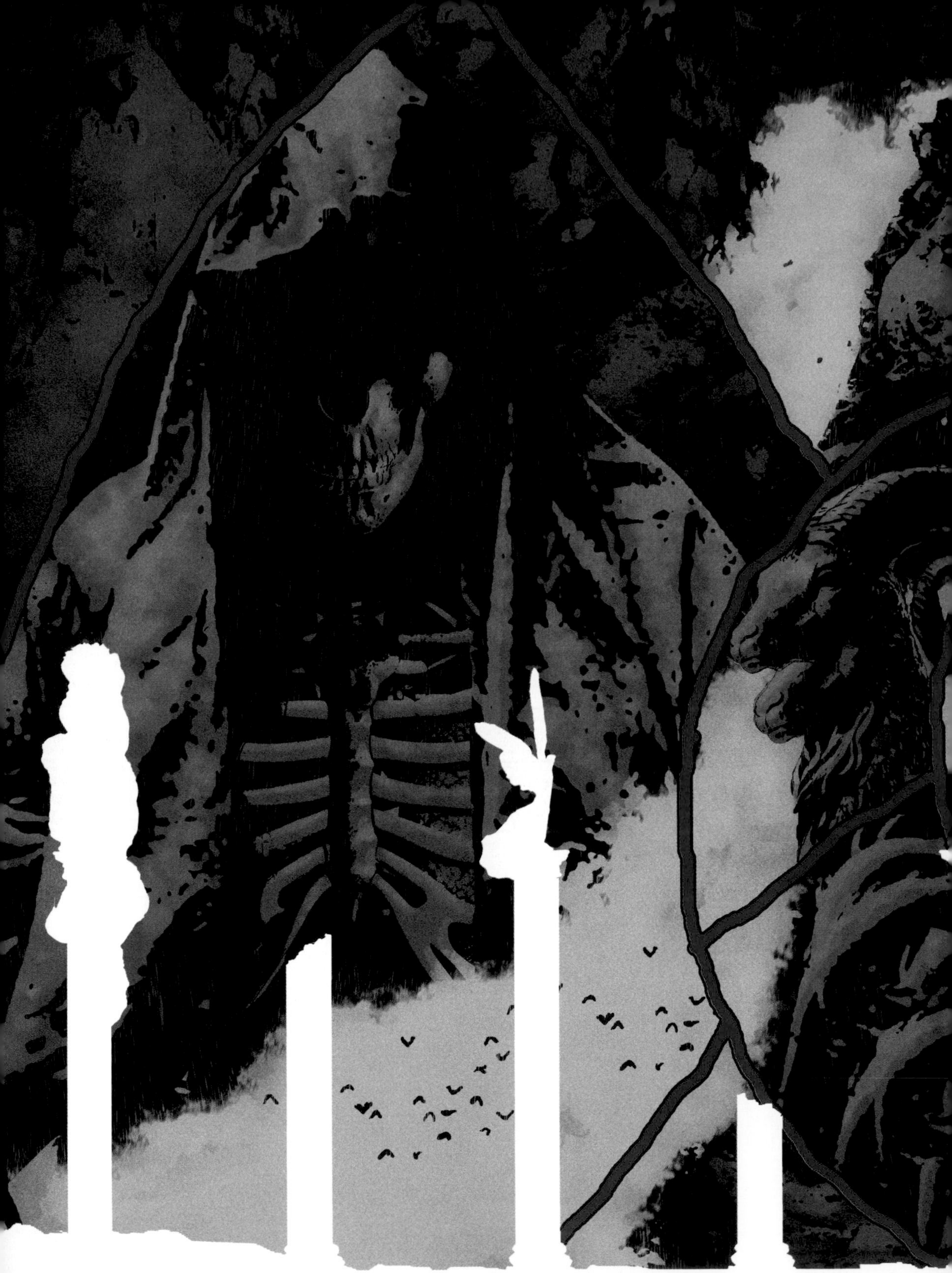

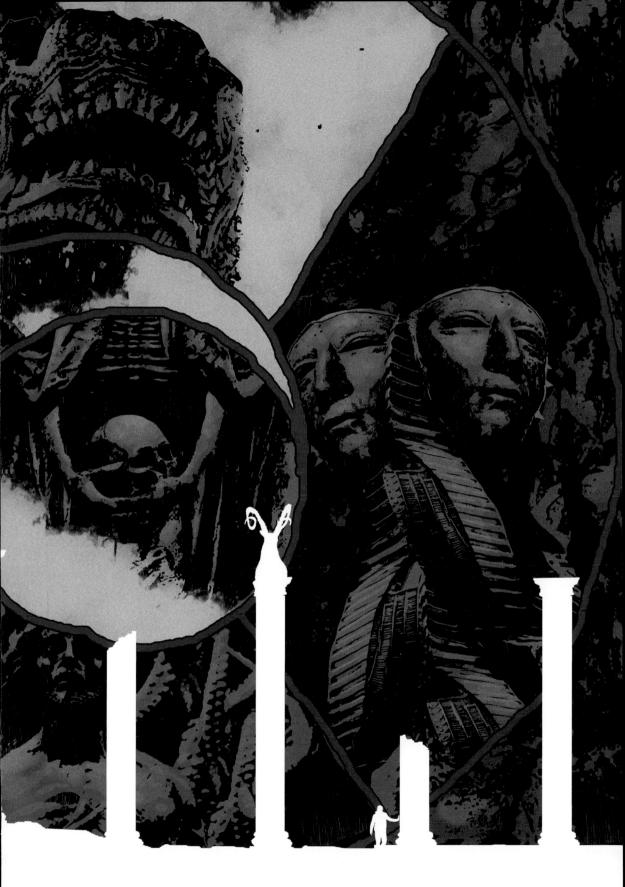

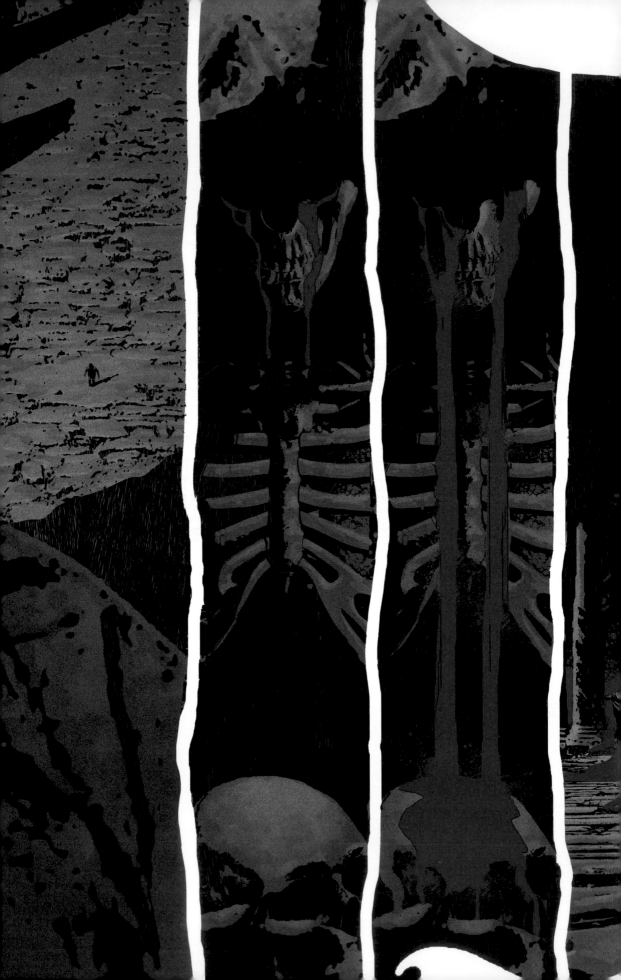

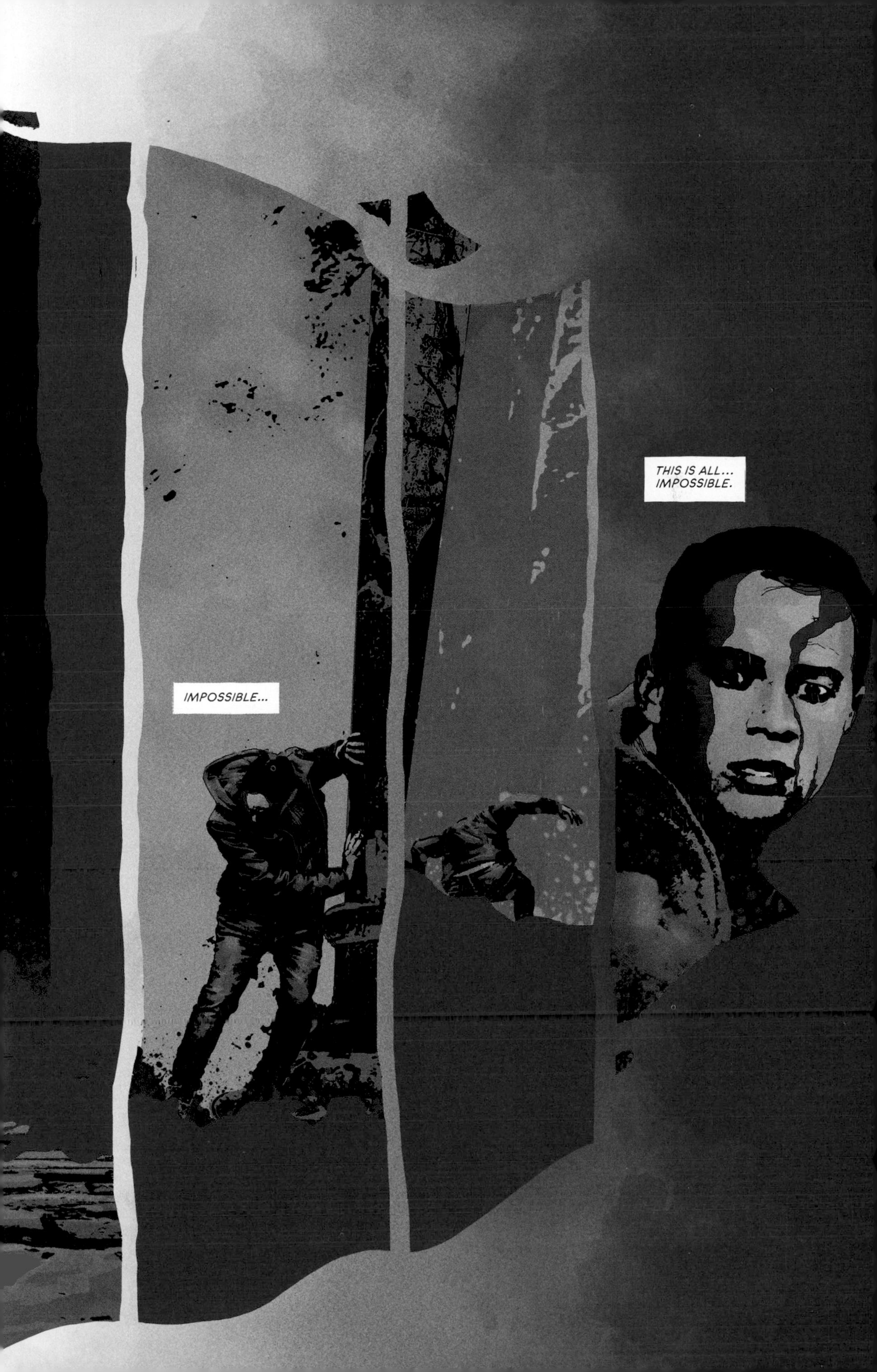
THIS IS ALL... IMPOSSIBLE.
IMPOSSIBLE...

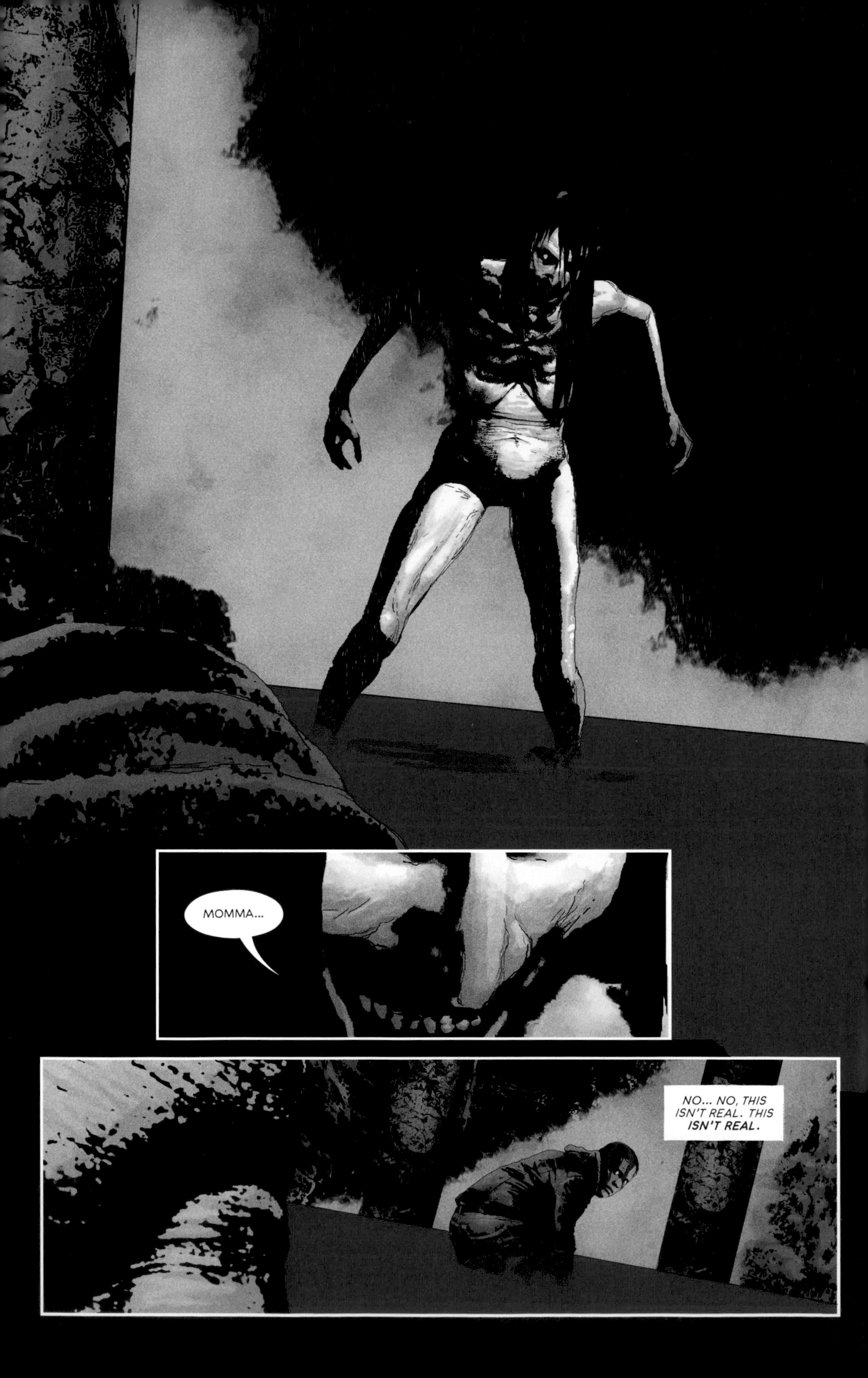
MOMMA...
NO... NO, THIS ISN'T REAL. THIS **ISN'T REAL.**

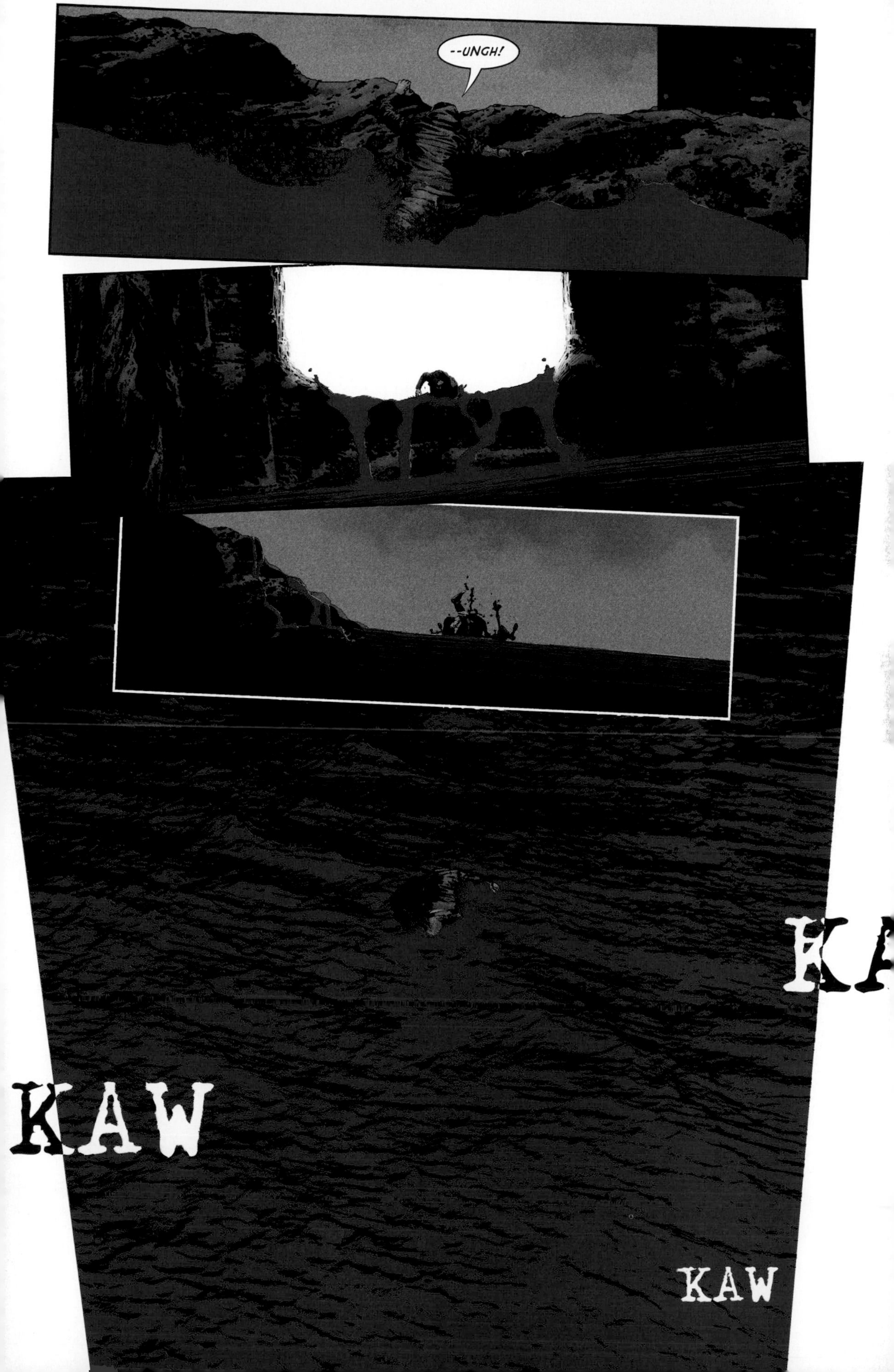
--UNGH!
KA
KAW
KAW

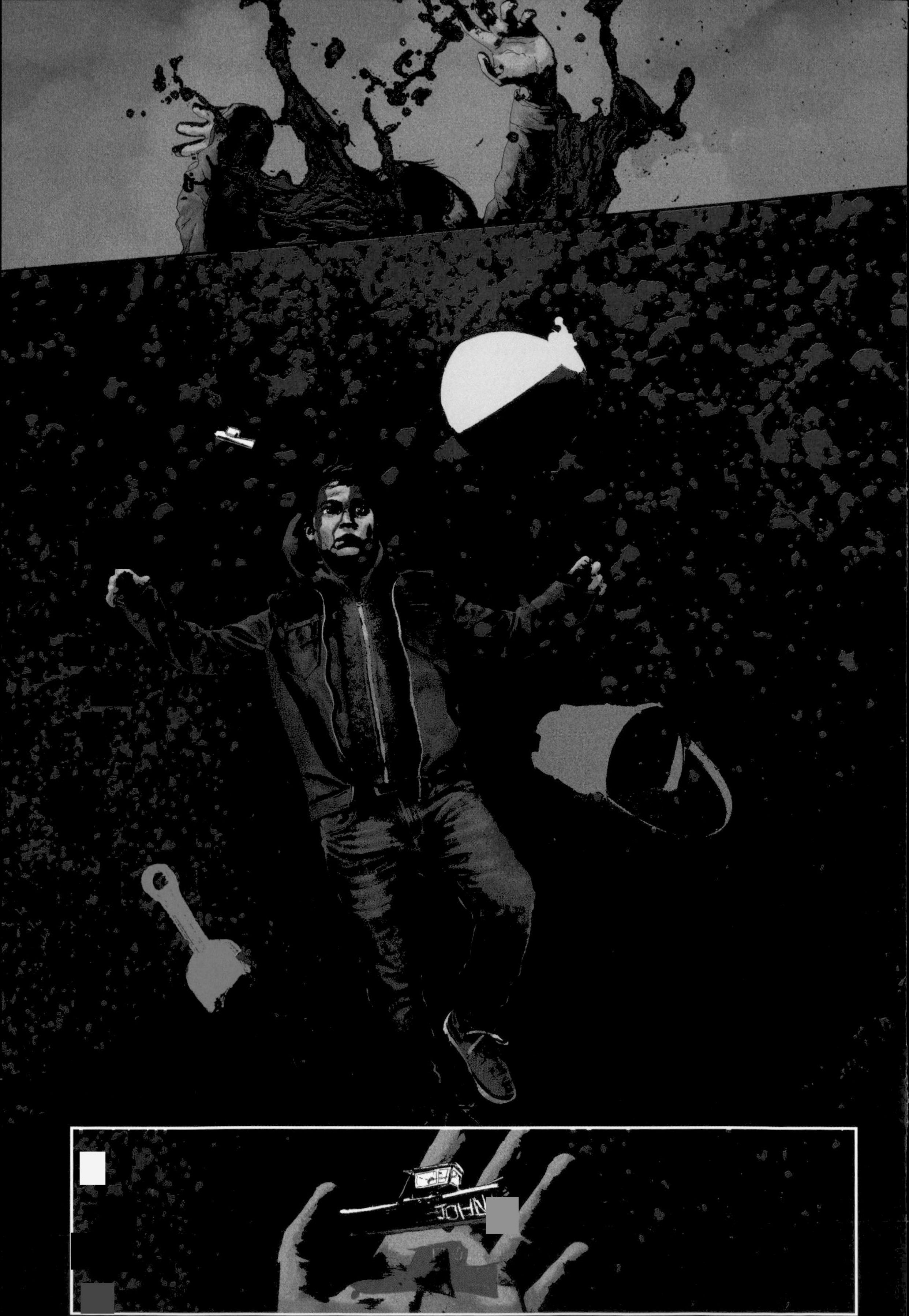
JOHN

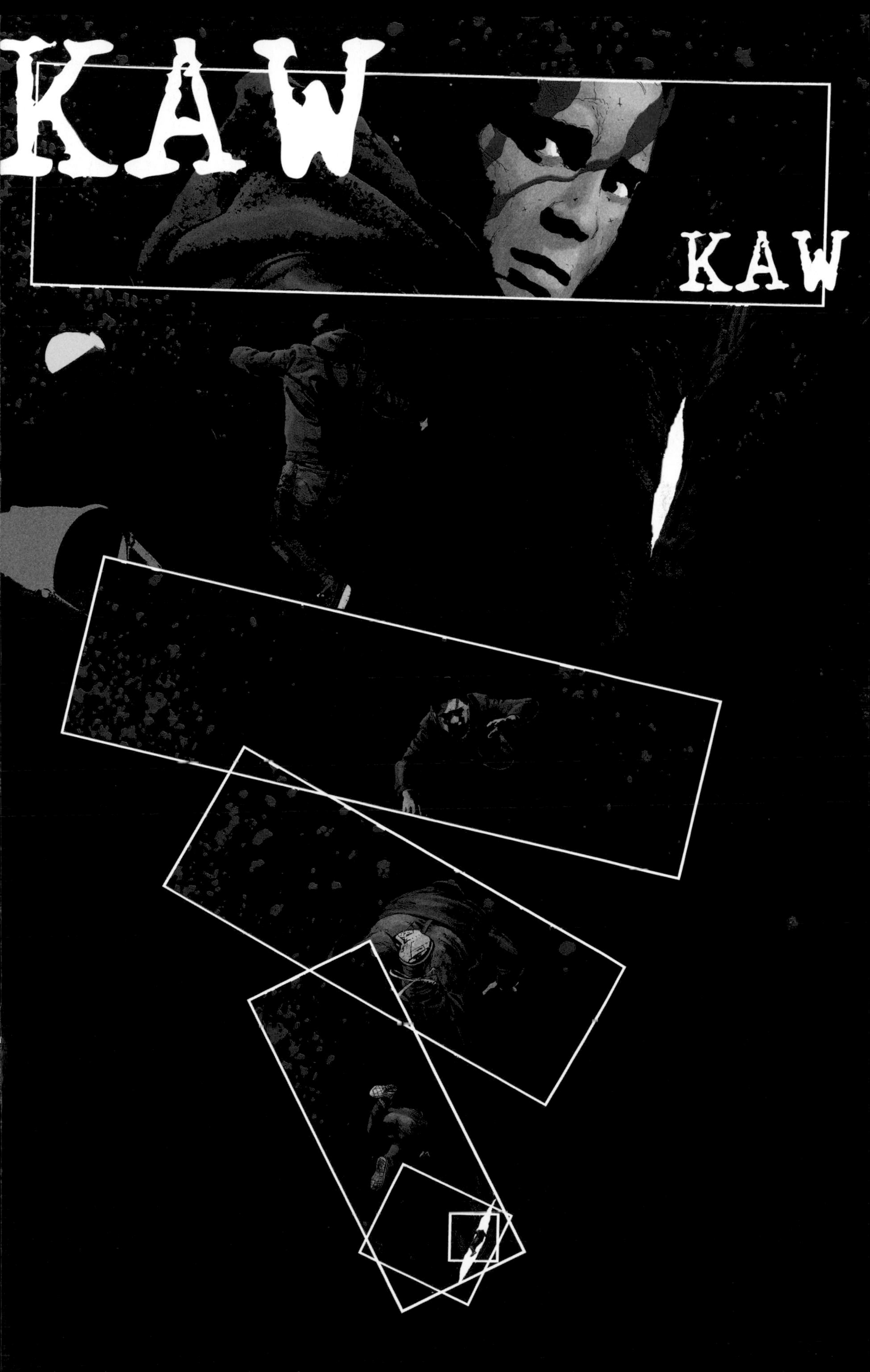
KAW
KAW

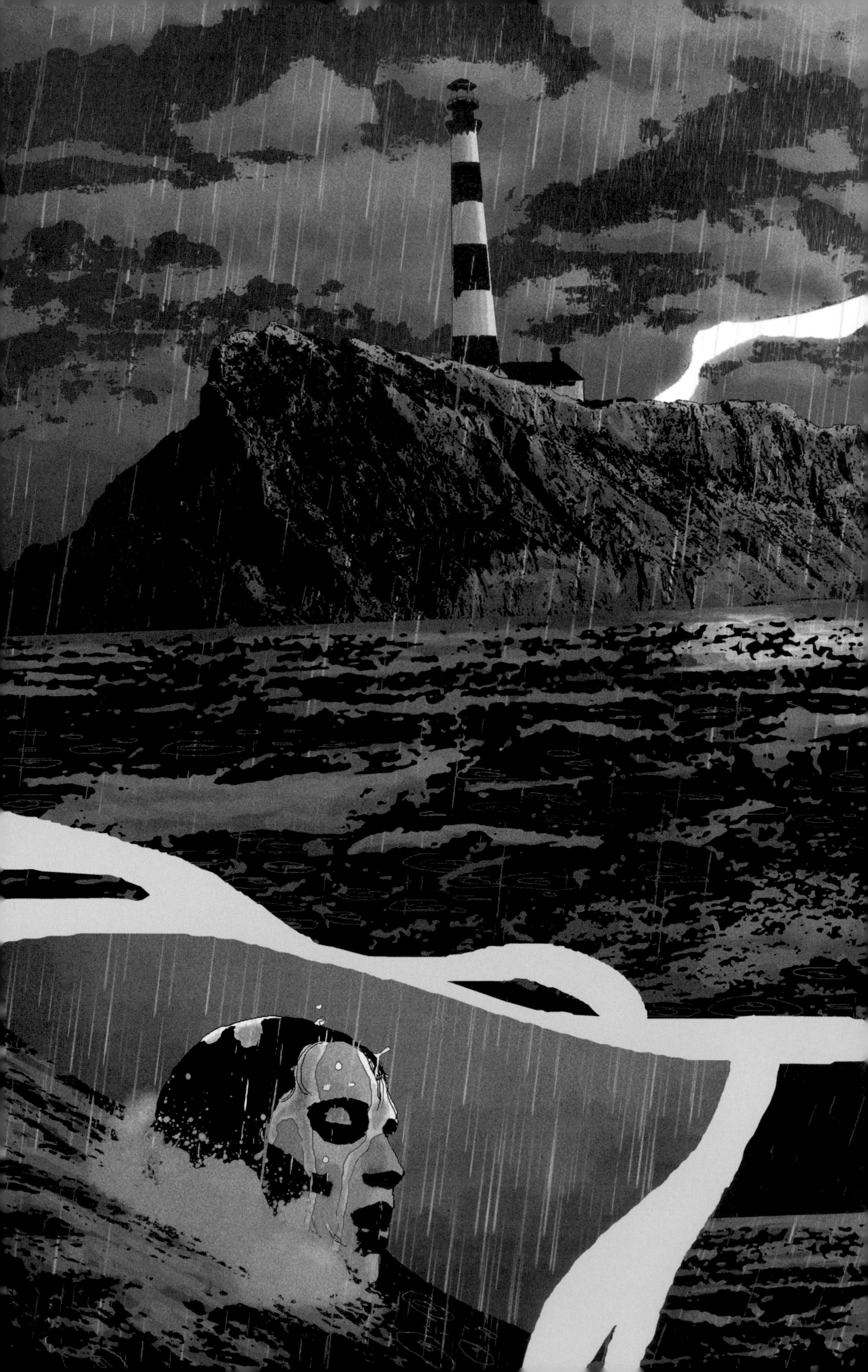

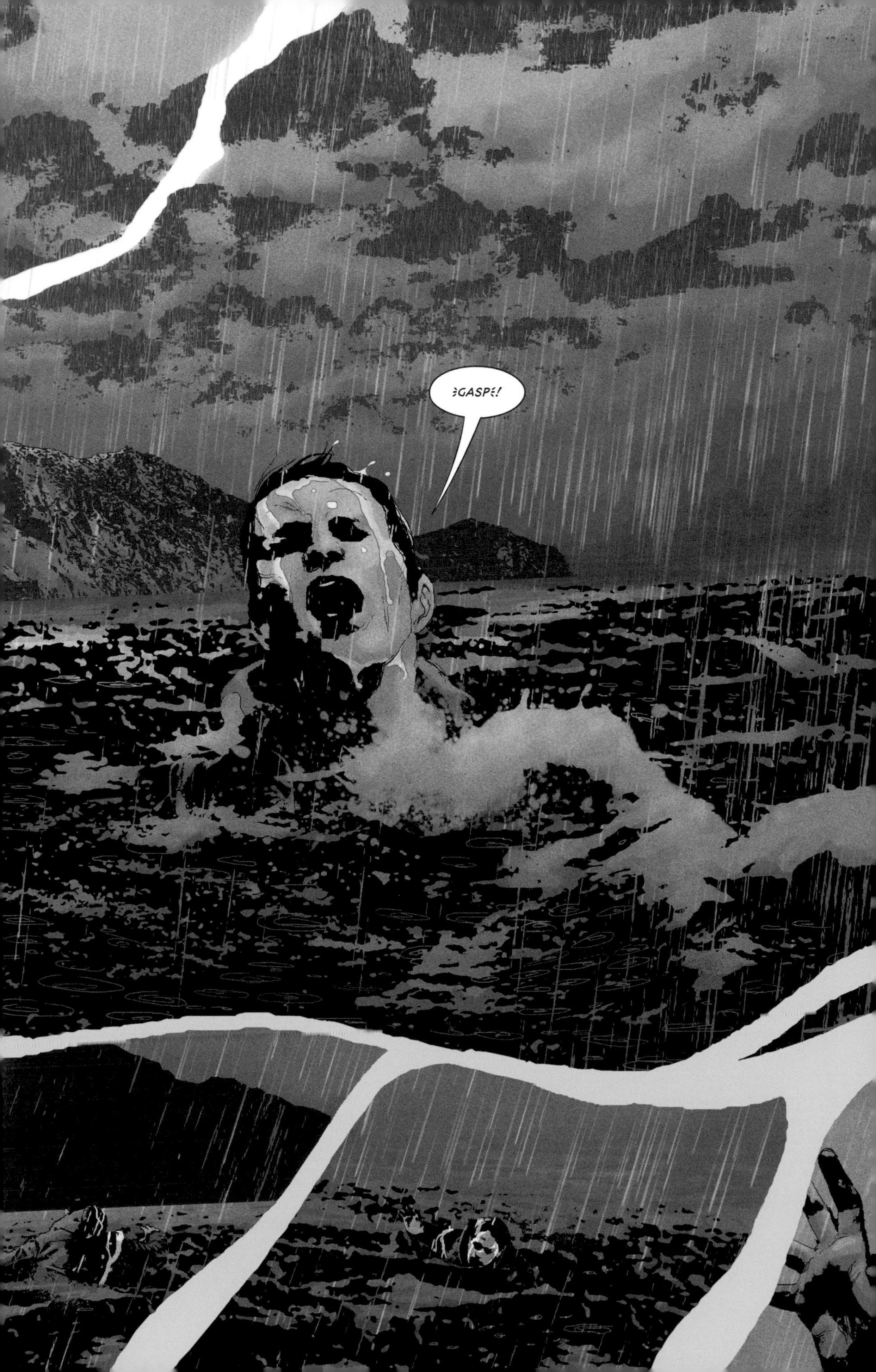
GASP!

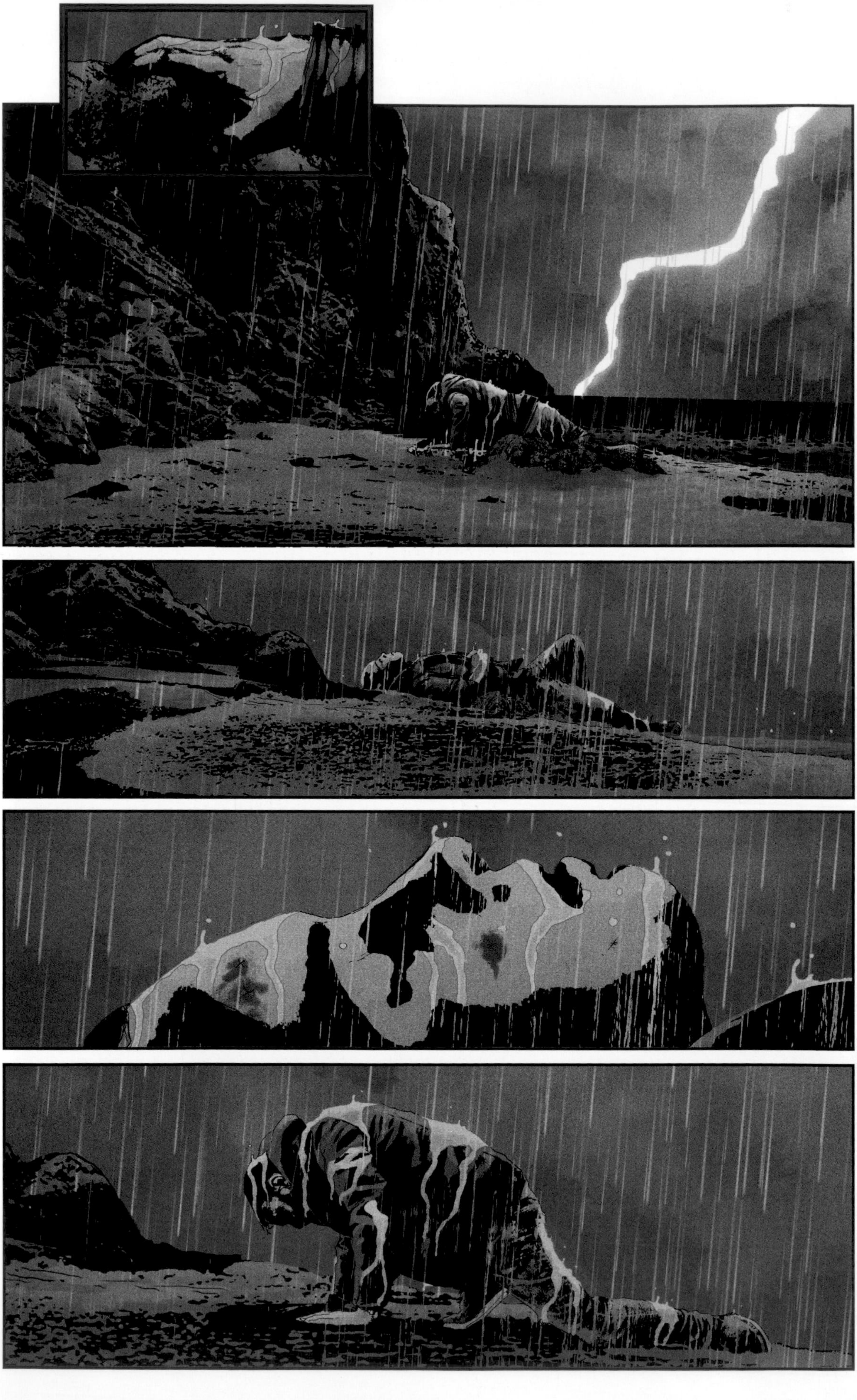

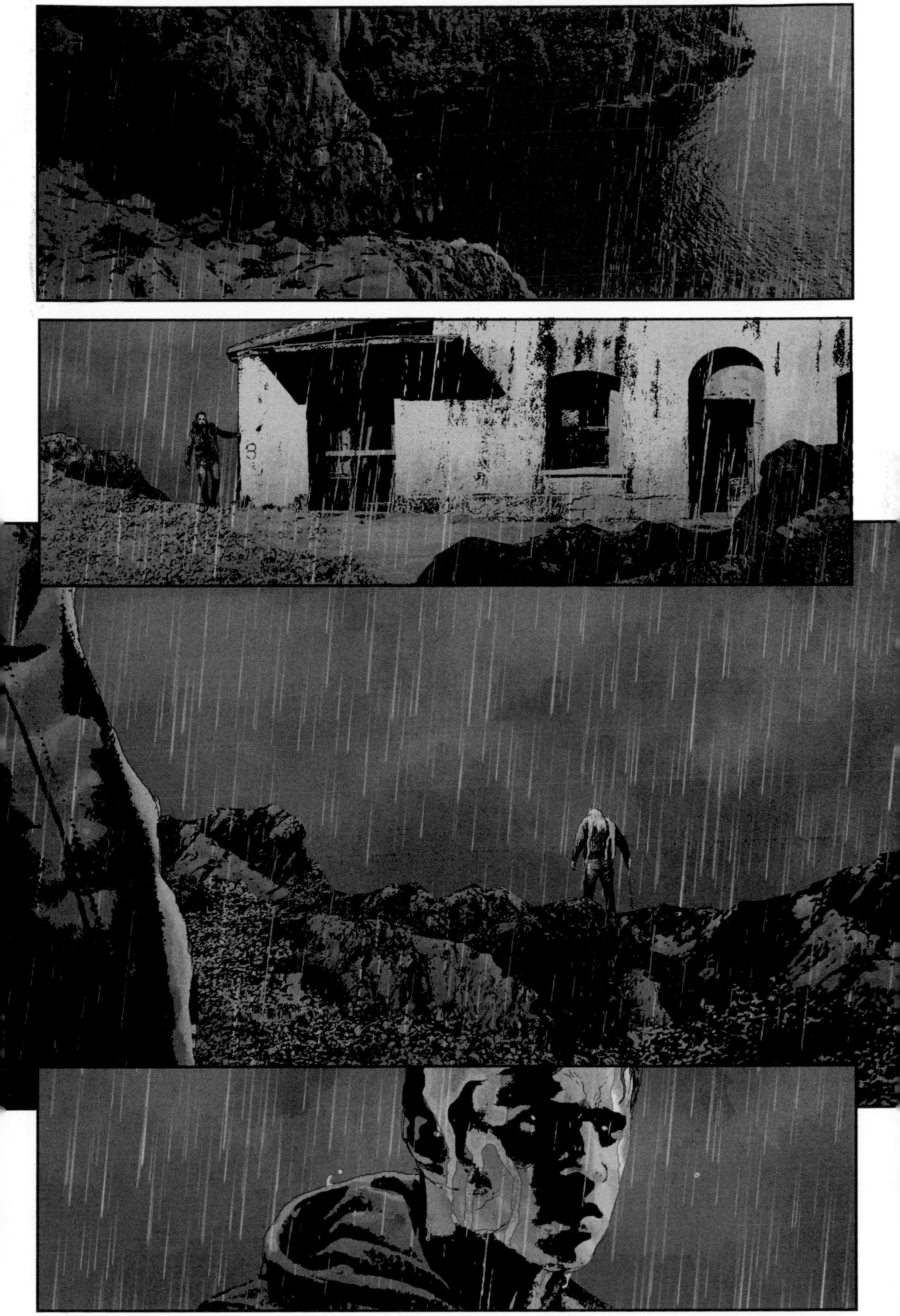

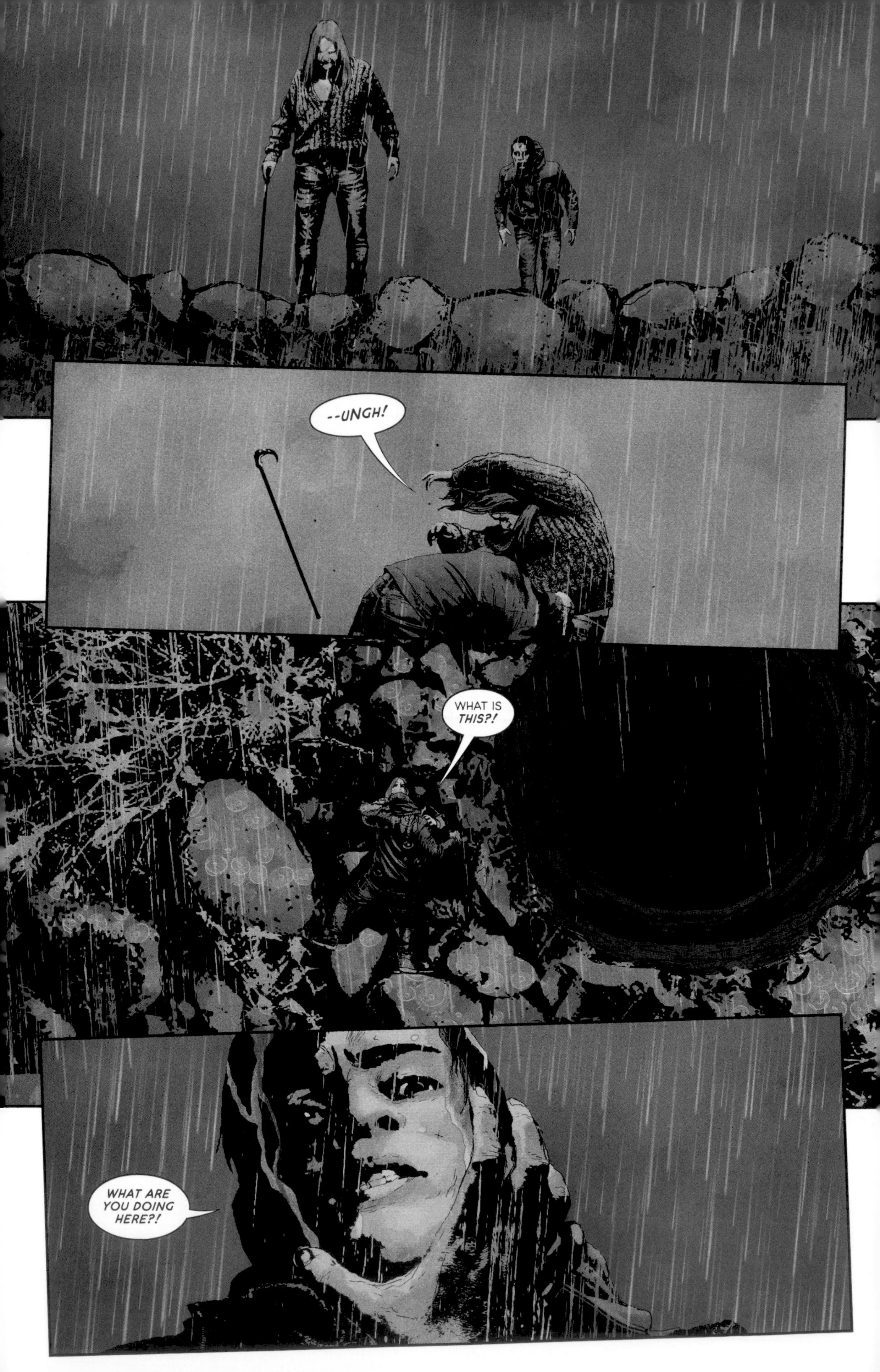
--UNGH!
WHAT IS THIS?!
WHAT ARE YOU DOING HERE?!

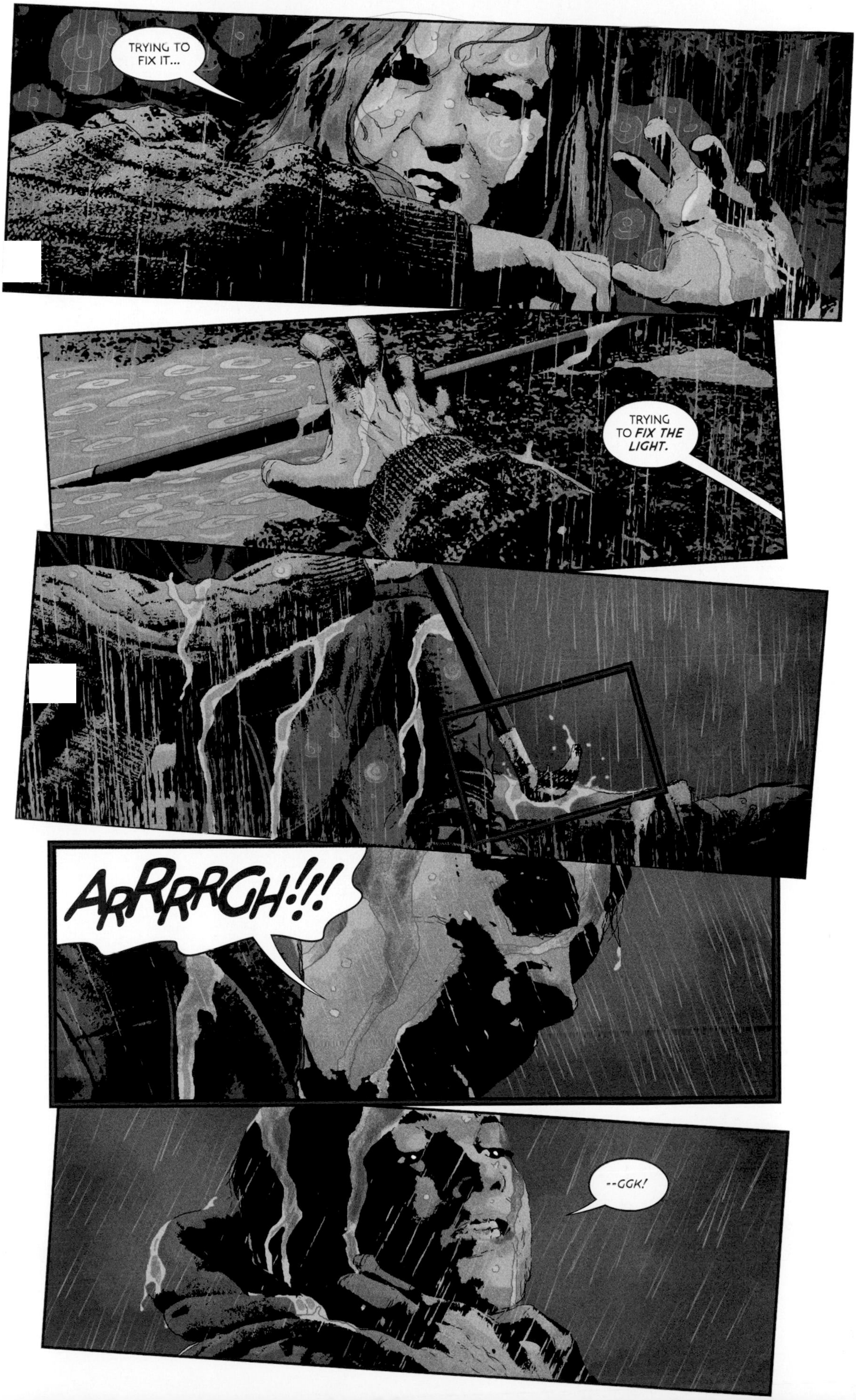
TRYING TO FIX IT...
TRYING TO *FIX THE LIGHT.*
ARRRRGH!!!
--GGK!

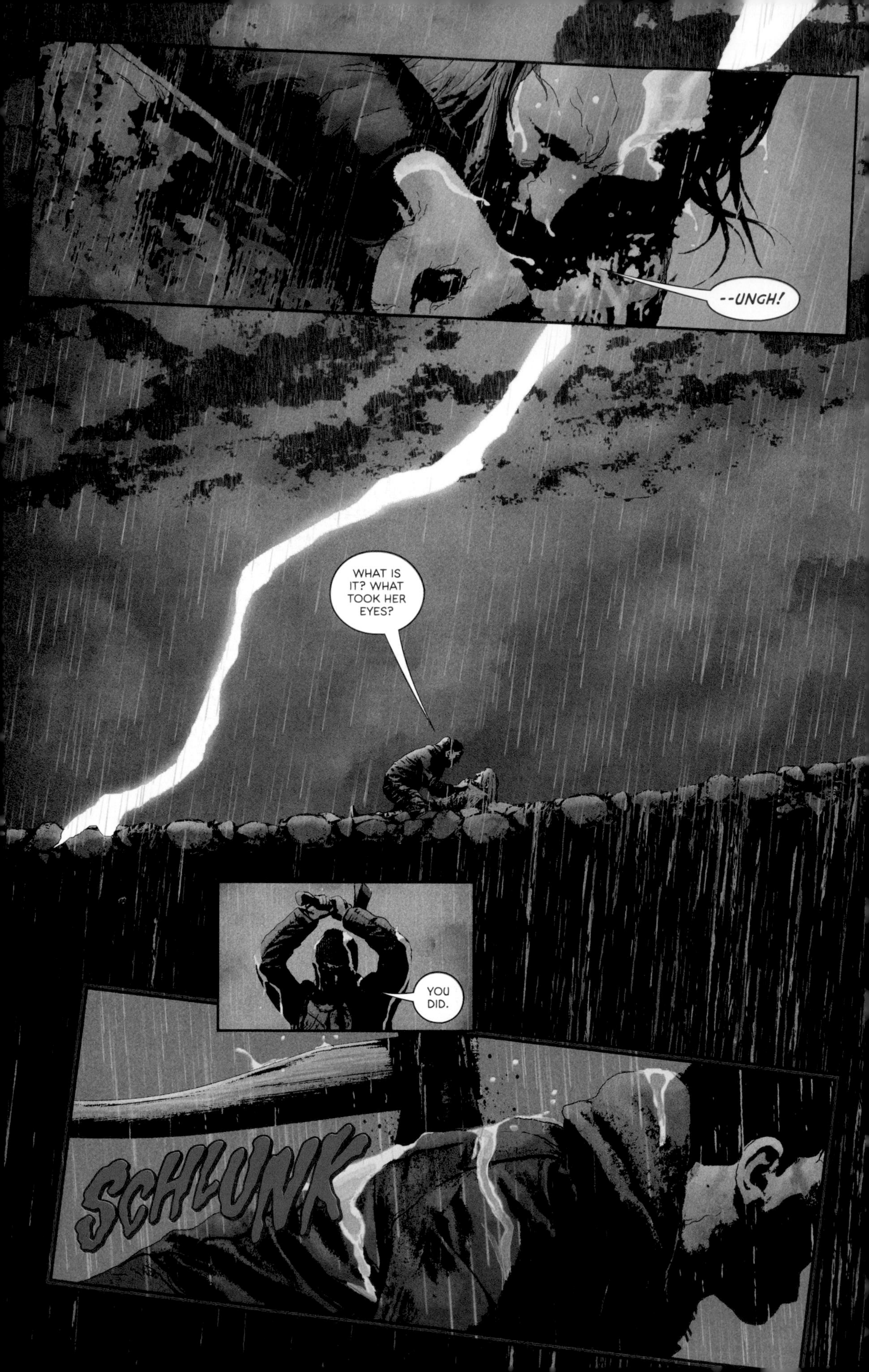
--UNGH!
WHAT IS IT? WHAT TOOK HER EYES?
YOU DID.
SCHLUNK

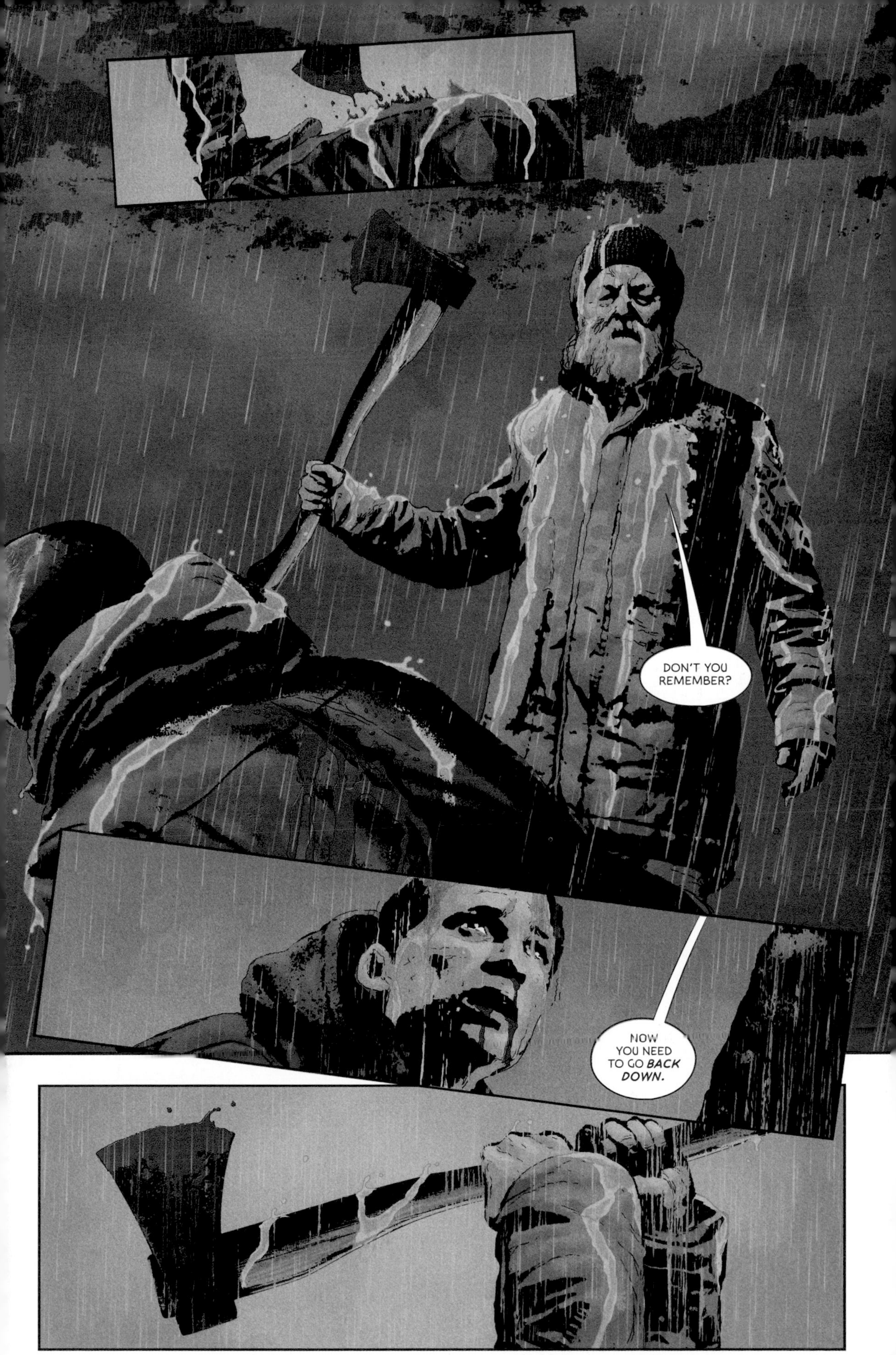
DON'T YOU REMEMBER?
NOW YOU NEED TO GO *BACK DOWN.*

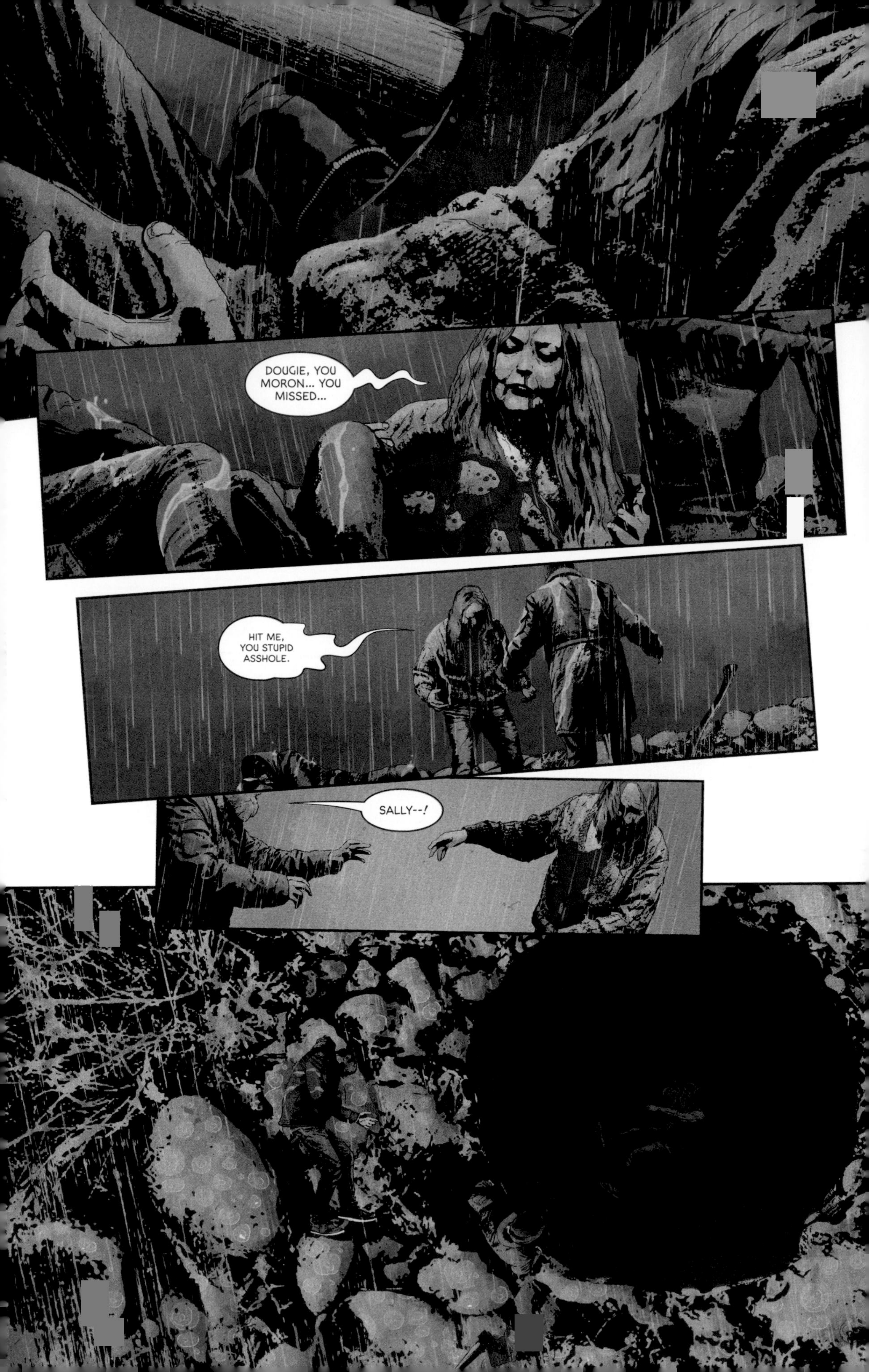
DOUGIE, YOU MORON... YOU MISSED...
HIT ME, YOU STUPID ASSHOLE.
SALLY--!

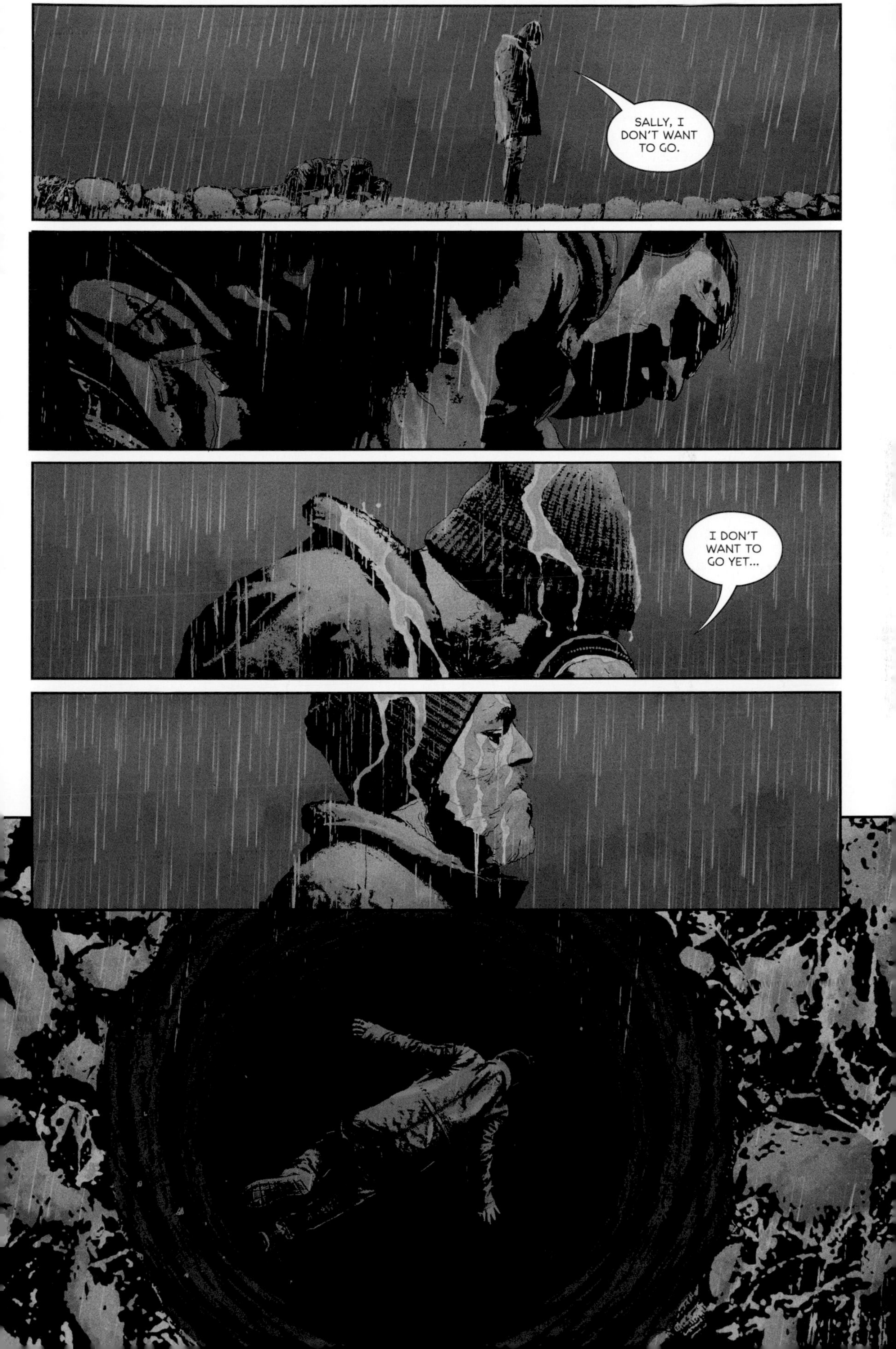
SALLY, I DON'T WANT TO GO.
I DON'T WANT TO GO YET...

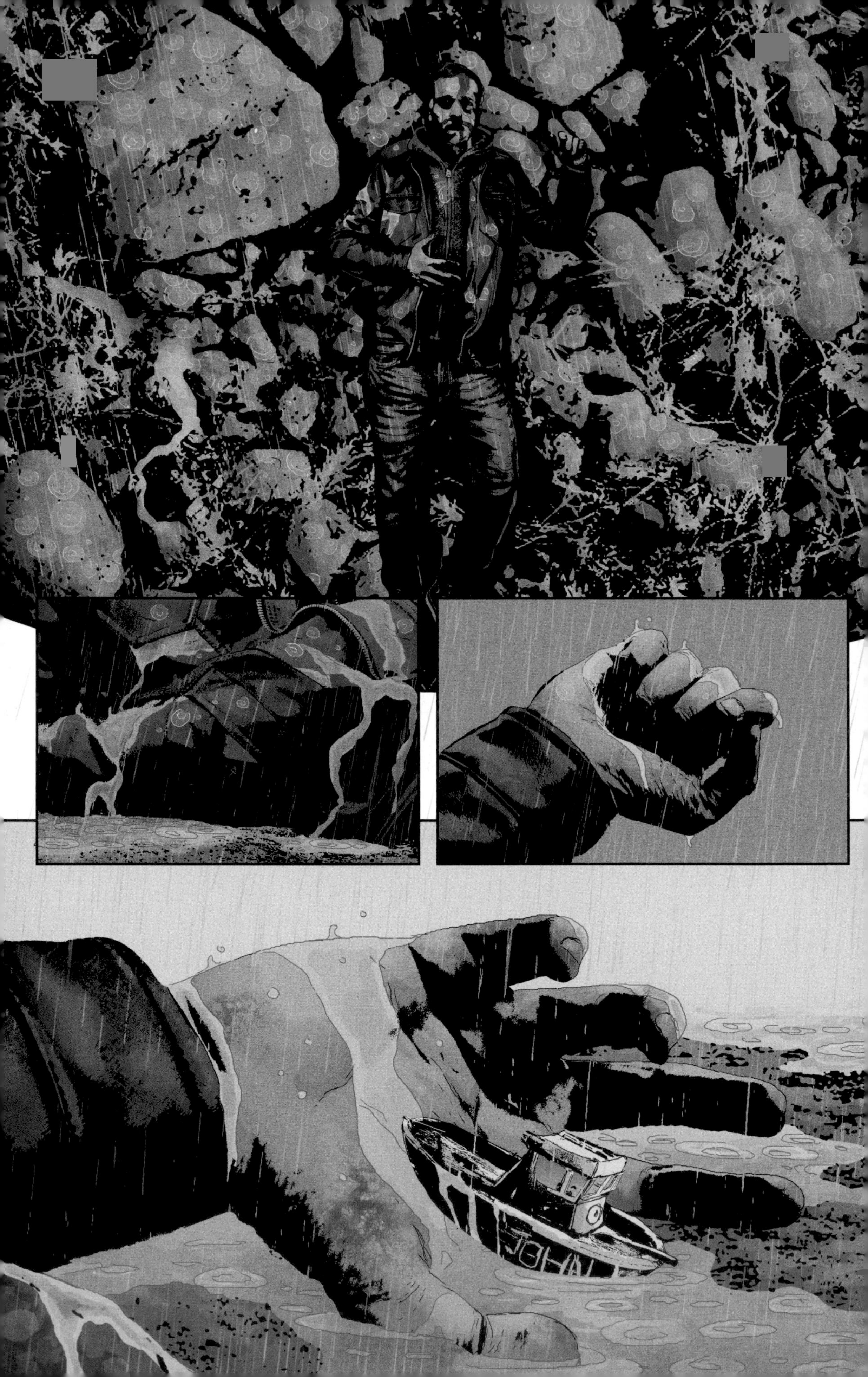

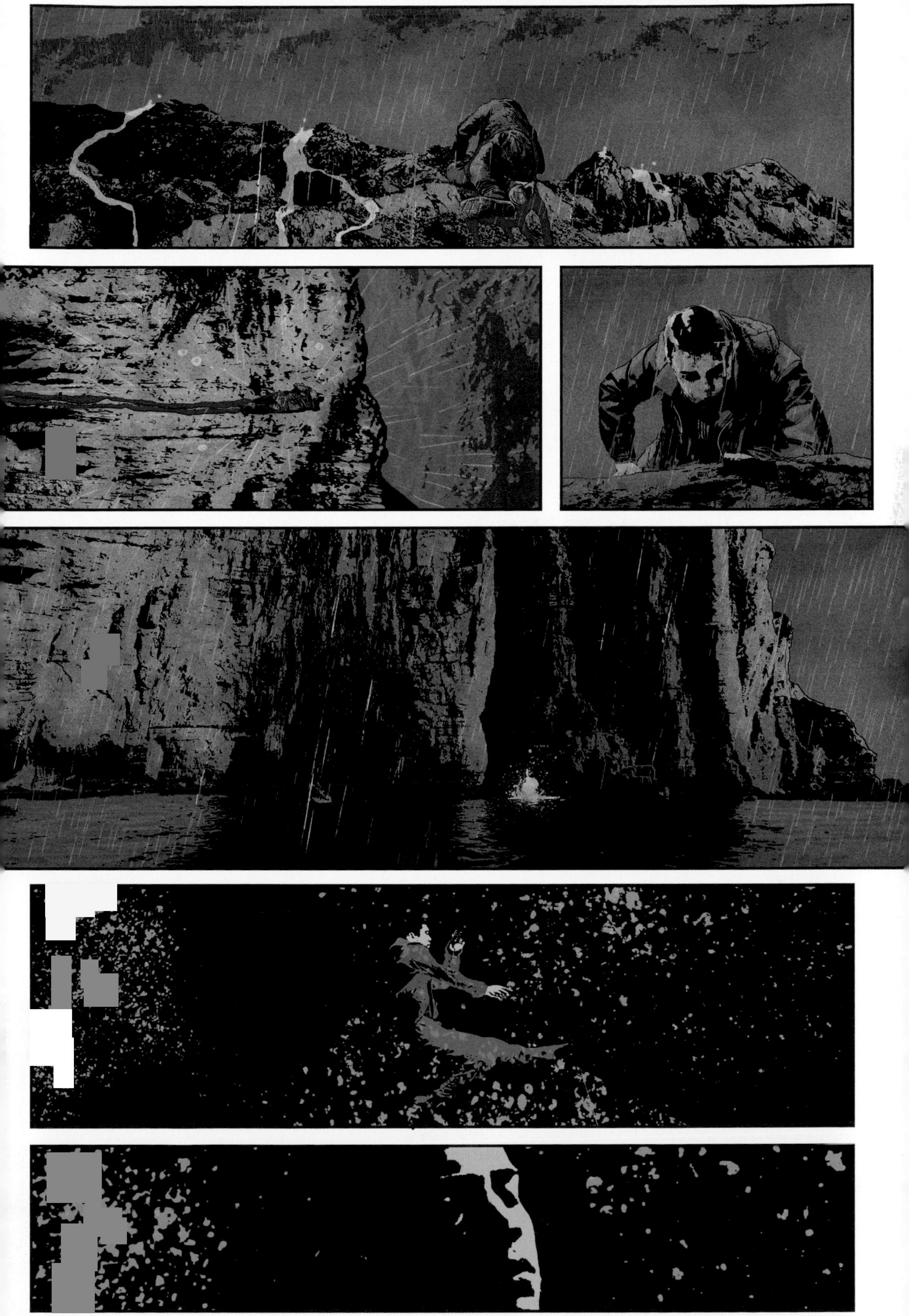

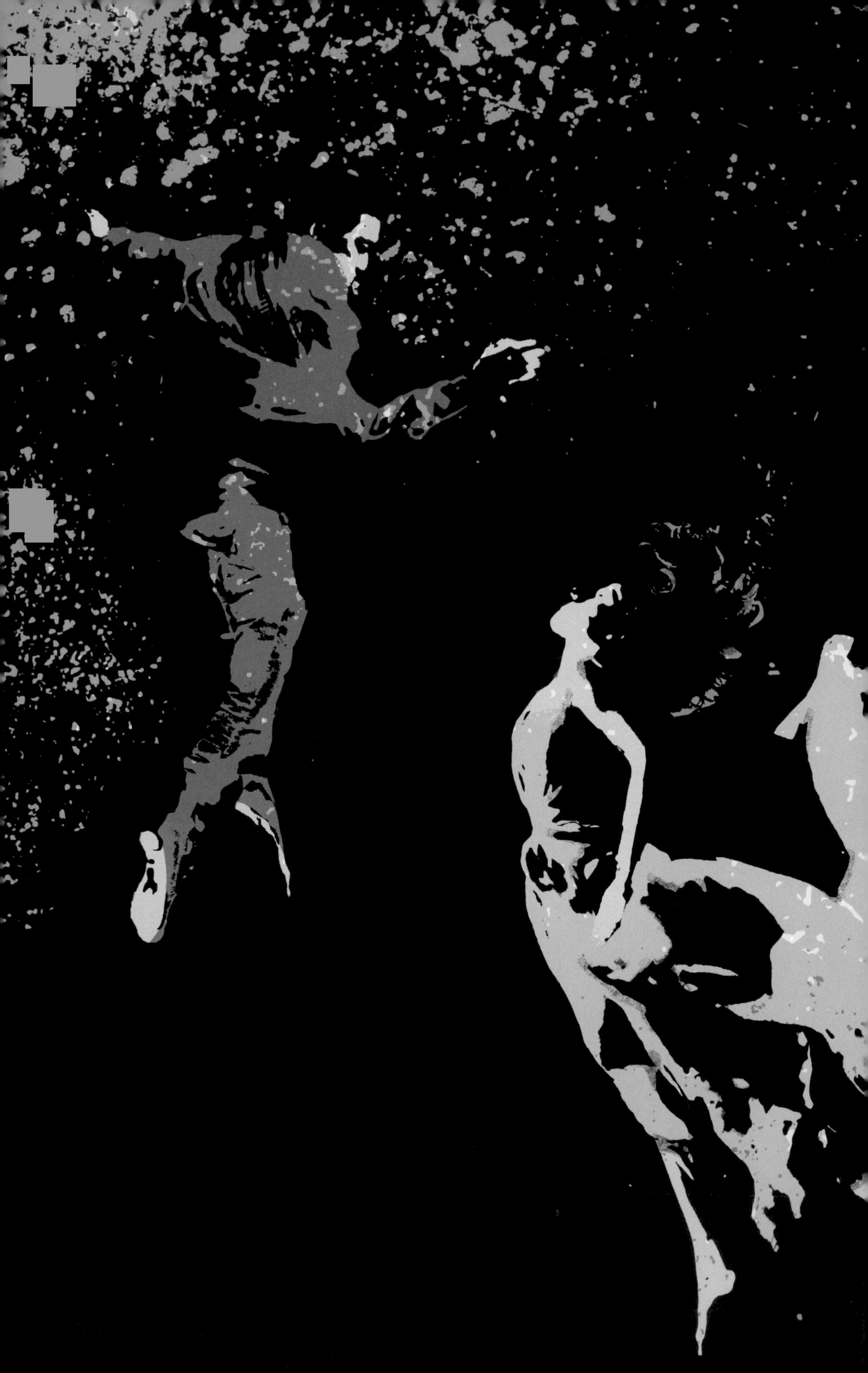

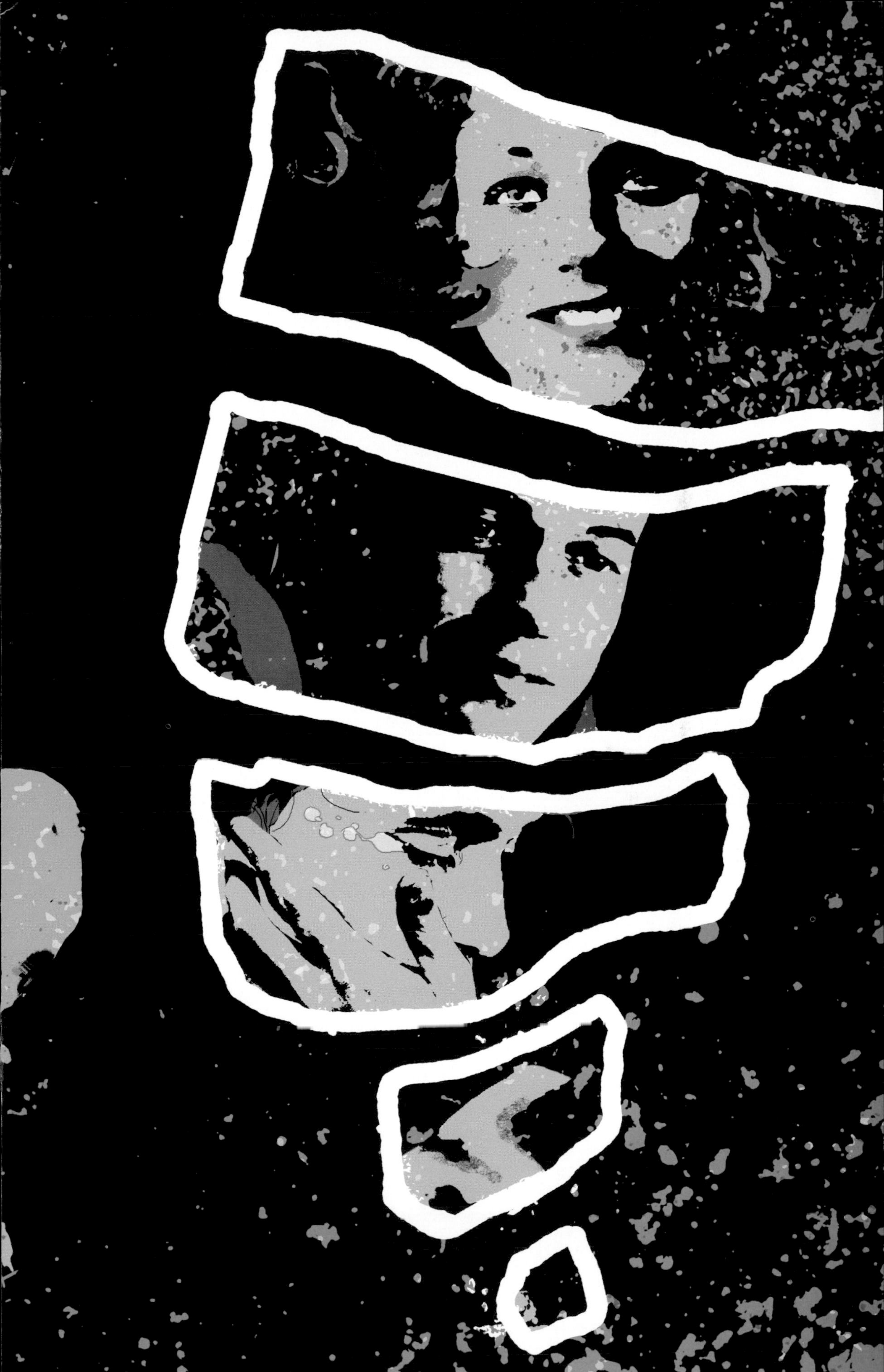

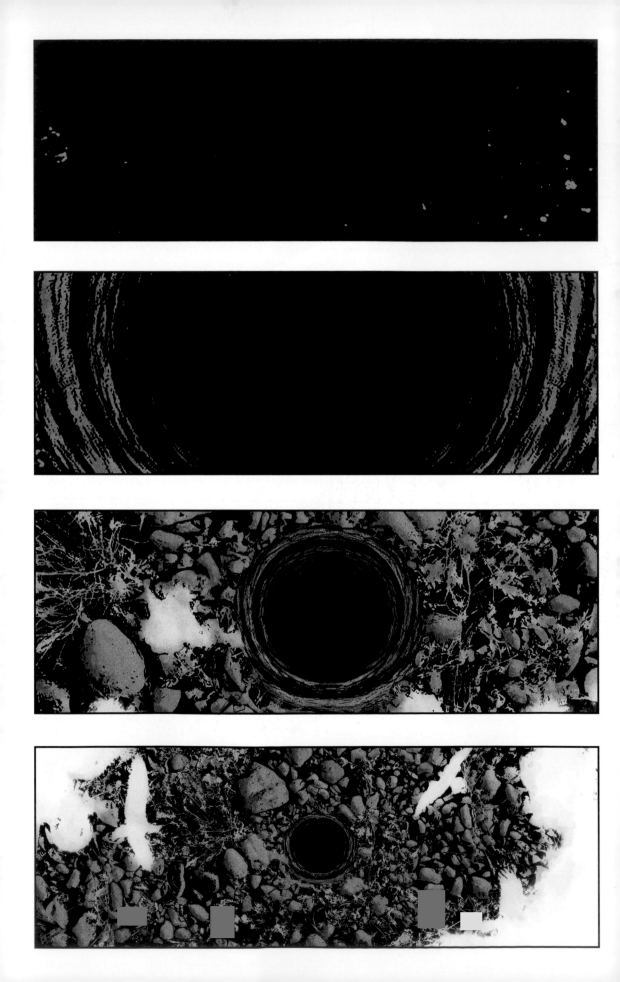

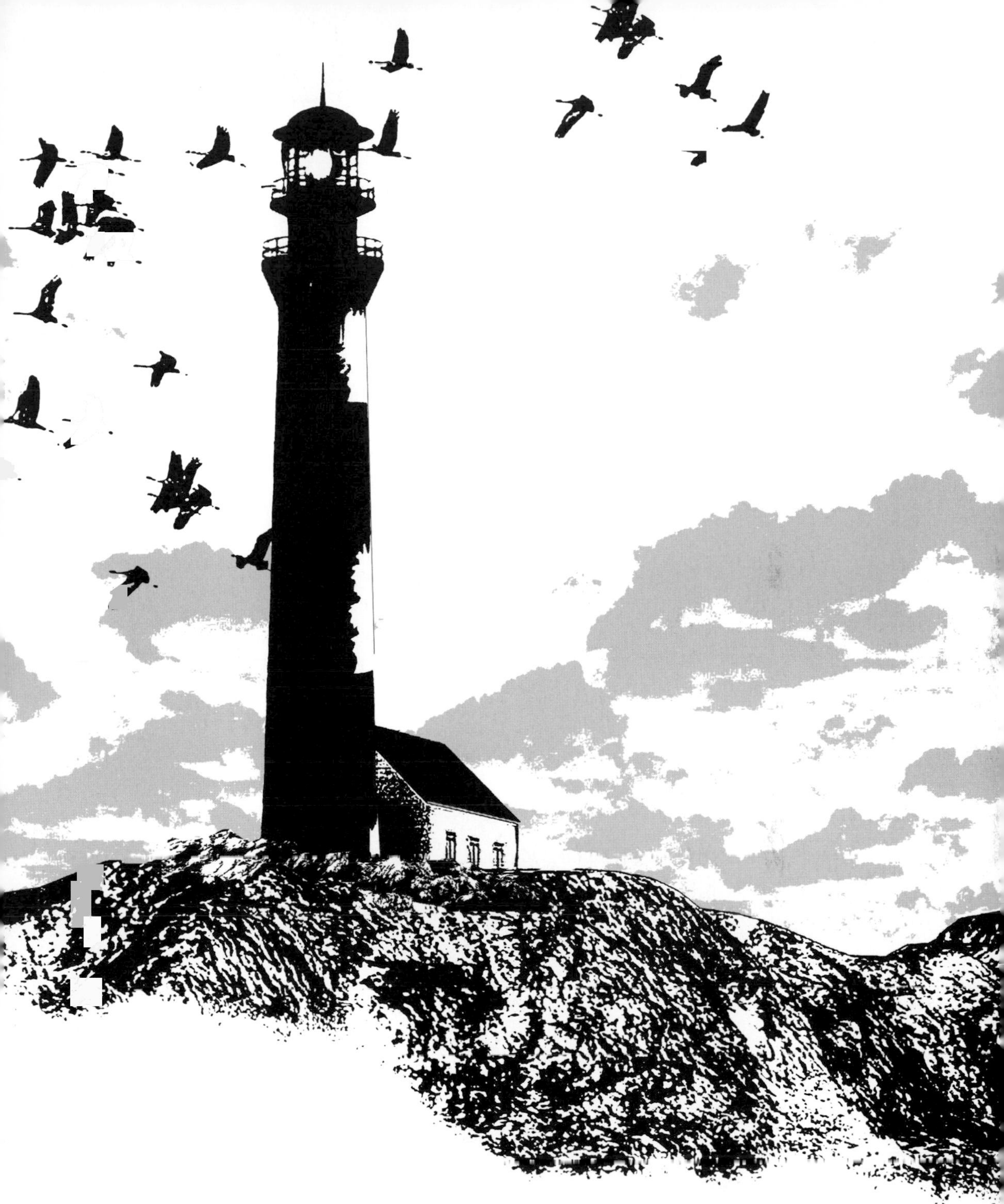

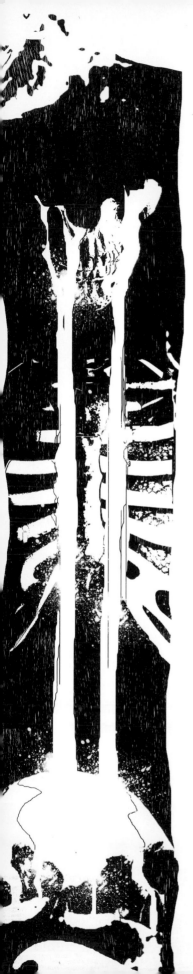

JEFF LEMIRE

is the creator of the acclaimed graphic novels *Sweet Tooth* (at Netflix from Robert Downey Jr.), the *Essex County Trilogy*, *The Underwater Welder*, *Trillium* and *Roughneck*, as well as *Descender* and *Ascender* with Dustin Nguyen and *Black Hammer* with Dean Ormston. Jeff has also written *Green Arrow*, *Justice League* and *Animal Man* for DC Comics and *Hawkeye* for Marvel Comics. He's also part of the creative team on *Cosmic Detective*, which he recently Kickstarted with Matt Kindt and David Rubín.

In 2008 and in 2013 Jeff won the Shuster Award for Best Canadian Cartoonist. He has also received the Doug Wright Award for Best Emerging Talent and the American Library Association's prestigious Alex Award, recognizing books for adults with specific teen appeal. He has also been nominated for 8 Eisner awards, 7 Harvey Awards and 8 Shuster Awards. In 2010 *Essex County* was named as one of the five Essential Canadian Novels of the Decade. He currently lives and works in Toronto with his wife and son.

ANDREA SORRENTINO

is the artist and co-creator of the critically praised and Eisner Award-winning *Gideon Falls* as well as the artist of other DC and Marvel hits like *Joker: Killer Smile*, *Batman: The Imposter* and *Wolverine: Old Man Logan*. He's renowned in the comic world for his tense, moody and suspenseful art and creative layouts that go beyond beat-to-beat storytelling and into evocations of deep, suggestive mental states.

Sorrentino lives and works just outside of Naples, Italy, precariously close to an active volcano.

DAVID STEWART

has worked as a colorist for over 20 years. He's worked on titles like *Hellboy*, *Shaolin Cowboy*, *Black Hammer* and *Ultramega*. He resides in Portland, Oregon with his wife and three black cats.

STEVE WANDS

is best known as a Harvey Award-nominated and Lammy Award-winning comic book Letterer with DC Comics, Image, TKO Studios, Dark Horse and others, but he's also indie author of the *Stay Dead* series, *Night of the Drunks* and co-writer of *Trail of Blood*. When not working, he spends time with his family in New Jersey.

GREG LOCKARD

is a comic book writer and editor. As a freelance editor, his clients have included ComiXology Originals, Image Comics, Einhorn's Epic Productions and others. As a member of the Vertigo editorial staff, he worked on a number of critically acclaimed titles including *Dial H*, *The Unwritten*, *Sweet Tooth* and many others. *Liebestrasse*, published by ComiXology Originals, is his debut graphic novel as a writer and co-creator.

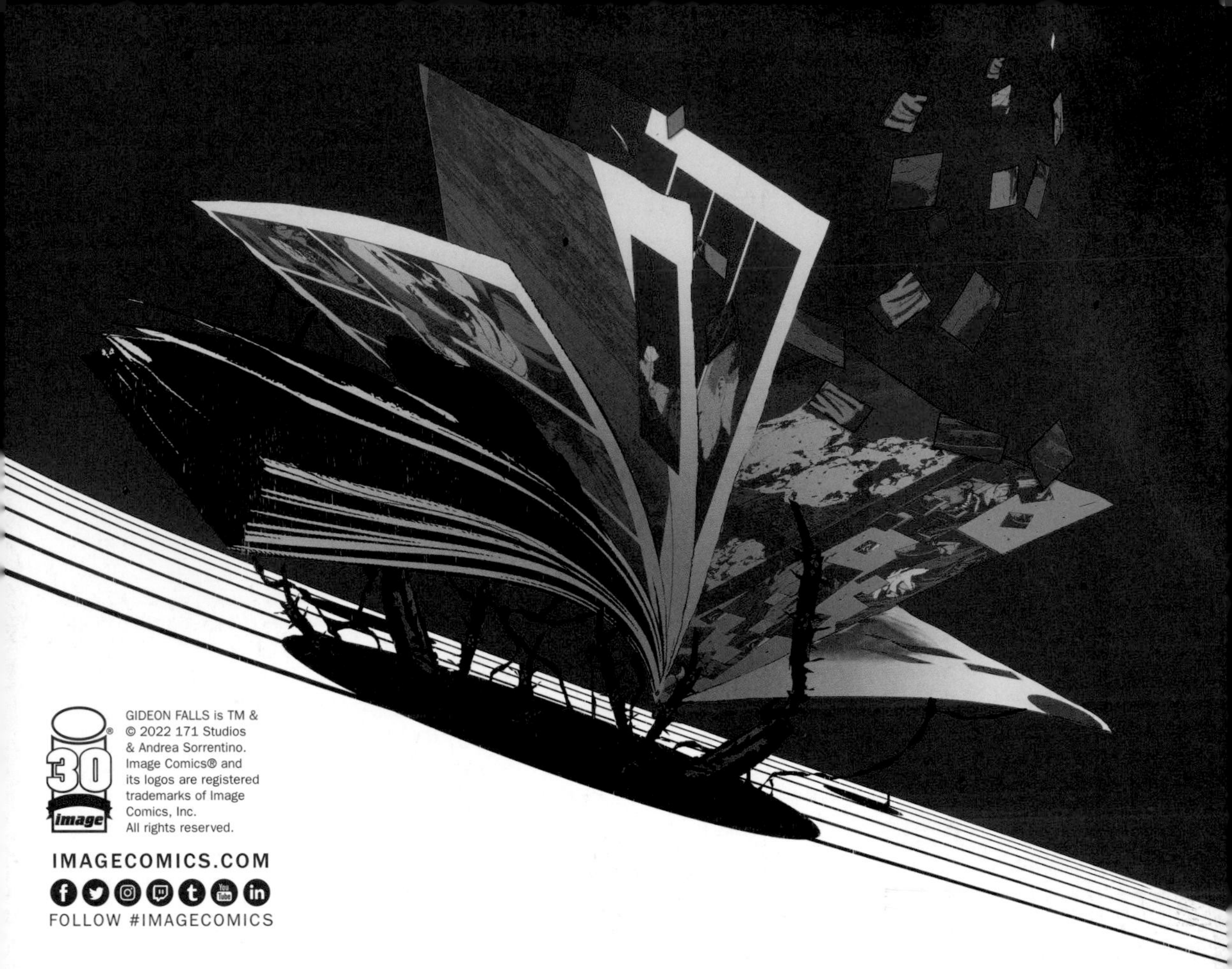

TERROR THROUGH TIME AND SPACE

GIDEON FALLS™

Experience the groundbreaking horror series in its entirety.

Volumes one through six available now in trade paperback.

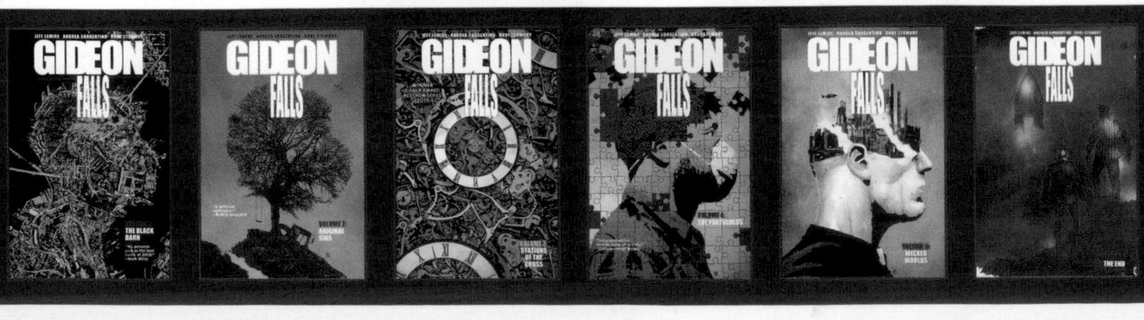
GIDEON FALLS
THE BLACK BARN
GIDEON FALLS
GIDEON FALLS
STATIONS OF THE CROSS
GIDEON FALLS
GIDEON FALLS
WICKED WORLDS
GIDEON FALLS
THE END